FREUD

The Psychoanalytic Adventure

DRAWINGS BY
Michel Siméon

TEXT BY
Robert Ariel

FREUD
The Psychoanalytic Adventure

TRANSLATED FROM THE FRENCH BY
ROBERT C. WHITE

Holt, Rinehart and Winston
NEW YORK

The authors of this book wish to acknowledge their debt to the
monumental and indispensable biography of Freud by Ernest Jones,
The Life and Work of Sigmund Freud, 1953, 1955, 1957 (Basic Books),
without which their work could not have been accomplished.

Library of Congress Cataloging in Publication Data

Siméon, Michel.
    Freud: the psychoanalytic adventure.

    Translation of Freud: l'aventure psychanalytique.
    1. Psychoanalysis—Caricatures and cartoons.
2. Freud, Sigmund, 1856–1939—Cartoons, satire, etc.
I. Ariel, Robert, joint author. II. Title.
BF175.S55413   150′.19′520207   77–29220
ISBN : 0–03–021696–6

First published in the United States in 1978.

Printed in the United States of America

10 9 8 7 6 5 4 3 2 1

A long trek lasting several centuries—this seems to be the very ordinary history of a Jewish family named Freud who settled in Moravia in the nineteenth century. But mounting economic difficulties and portents of further persecution would soon make this an uncertain sanctuary. The adversity imposed upon his ancestors is only hinted at in this account of everlasting impermanence, written by a man who was destined to die in London: "I have reason to believe that my father's family were settled for a long period in the Rhineland (at Cologne), that they fled to the east, and that they retraced their steps from Lithuania through Galicia to German Austria."

Freiberg, near the border of Silesia, had a glorious past. Czech was still spoken by everyone except the hundred or so souls within the city's small Jewish enclave, who spoke Yiddish or German. It was there that Jakob Freud (1815–1896), son of Rabbi Schlomo, who was the son of Rabbi Ephraim, earned his living as best he could in the wool trade.

Jakob was a jovial man with a skeptical and liberal outlook; he was married at seventeen and sired two sons, Emmanuel and Philipp. After his first wife's death, he married Amalie Nathansohn, twenty years his junior, who gave him five daughters and three sons. At the time of his birth, May 6, 1856, Sigismund was an uncle. It is reasonably certain that his feelings of hostility, never openly displayed toward his father, were directed against his half brother Philipp and his nephew, Emmanuel's son.

Amalie was tenderly devoted to this son who was "born lucky" (he was born in a caul). At sixty-one, in an essay on Goethe, Freud confided the following autobiographical detail: "A man who has been the indisputable favorite of his mother keeps for life the feeling of a conqueror, that confidence of success that often induces real success."

If as a young man Freud was to see himself in a dream as cabinet minister, if at the moment of choosing a career he was drawn to jurisprudence, it was because all things seemed possible for a young brilliant studious Jew who was, moreover, the object of a limitless maternal affection.

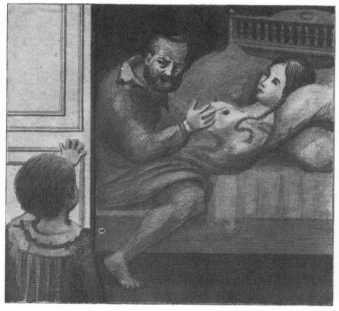

In the household of the young child there was also "that prehistoric old woman," the nurserymaid, Nannie, who spoke to him in Czech and took him with her to Mass. She was caught stealing, and Philipp insisted she be imprisoned. The incident left its mark on the child: he identified the "box" (prison) with the maternal womb, and thought in his confusion that Philipp was the father of his little sister Anna, whom he detested.

Like all children, young Freud strayed into his parents' bedroom, motivated by a keen sense of curiosity concerning sexual matters. But for him the essential mystery of birth was compounded, for he was not a little surprised to see a man nearing old age sharing the same bed with his mother, who was much more suited in years to Philipp.

The parents were often touched by the boy's childlike remarks, although the father was reprimanding. So it was when at the age of two the young lad wet his bed. It was from such experiences that Freud later would attest with great certainty that his father stood for the "reality principle" and his mother for the "pleasure principle."

But Jakob's business affairs were threatened by growing mechanization, inflation and, in 1859, the Austro-Italian War. Furthermore, Freiberg's decline was almost assured with the construction of a new railway which bypassed the town. There was widespread unemployment, accompanied by nationalism tinged with racism. In the eyes of the Czechs the real enemy quickly became the German-speaking Jews, who owned the textile plants. It was then that Jakob decided to assure his family's future elsewhere: first in Leipzig, then Vienna. Emmanuel went to Manchester, England, and became the object of Sigmund's envy (the name *Sigismund* would soon disappear in favor of the shortened form). These distressing uprootings left their mark on Freud's psychism for many years.

In his adult life, in dreams, Freud sometimes construed the inventory of his accomplishments and successes as compensation for a frightfully humiliating scene: when he was still very young, he willfully urinated in his parents' bedroom. Jakob, intent on creating an image as a responsible head of household, chastised the boy severely. But this recollection was offset by another: an old woman's prediction to his mother.

And still another prediction, recounted in *The Interpretation of Dreams*: "One evening, at a restaurant in the Prater, where my parents were accustomed to take me when I was eleven or twelve years of age, we noticed a man who was going from table to table and, for a small sum, improvising verses upon any subject given to him. I was sent to bring the poet to our table and, showing his gratitude, he threw off a few rhymes about myself, and

told us that I should probably one day become a cabinet minister. I can still distinctly remember the impression produced by this second prophecy. It was in the days of the *Bürger* Ministry, which even included some Jews. We illuminated the house in their honor. . . ." Freud's interest in politics would remain sporadic, however; we shall see in what circumstances it was aroused.

Young Freud spent most of his time reading and studying. He particularly liked languages, and had a great fondness for Shakespeare, whom he began reading at age eight. His life was marked by incessant intellectual discussions. To his thorough grounding in German culture was added his brilliance as a scholar, affording him unlimited opportunities.

Like most adolescents, he identified with many historic figures, one of whom was a curious choice, but not difficult to explain: Masséna, the general of the French Empire who was thought to be Jewish and who, Freud believed, was born on his birthday, a hundred years earlier. Also, Masséna had served under Napoleon, the liberator of the Jews of Central Europe.

When the war of 1870 began, Freud had just turned fourteen, and his dreams of becoming a great general gradually faded. That same year his nephew John visited the family in Vienna. In front of the other children, the two of them acted a scene adapted from Schiller, with Sigmund playing the role of the tyrannicide Brutus, who also figures in the story as having murdered his father.

Owing to many things, including the translation of thirty-three lines from Sophocles' *Oedipus Rex* and his original style in written German, Freud culminated his secondary-school studies *summa cum laude*. Later, in a speech commemorating the fiftieth anniversary of his former *Gymnasium*, he would explore the lasting but ambiguous influence of those father figures, his teachers, on the students' intellectual inquiries.

Freud persistently devoted his energies to a single end, that of linking his own name with some great discovery. This preoccupation became both urgent and troublesome when it was time to choose a career. If the young graduate opted for medicine, it was not so much because of his vocational calling as it was his admiration for two towering intellectuals. By his own admission,

Jews admire brains more than bodies. If I had to choose between the two I should also put the intellect first.

Freud became "a therapist against his own will."

Freud "suddenly retreats from his search of power over men, and turns to the more sublime power over nature, through science, and decides to study biology. Power, prestige, and wealth should come to him only contingent to being a great scientist," according to his direct disciple Siegfried Bernfeld.

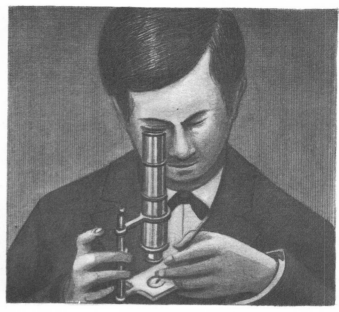

The decade between 1870 and 1880 marked the high point of Vienna's mania for science, a discipline already well established in other European countries and which seemed to offer enormous hopes. In the rigors of experimental science, Freud recognized the possibility of practicing self-restraint as a defense against his penchant for fantasy and abstract speculation.

Cleopatra's nose: During a vacation spent in Freiberg, Freud fell in love with a childhood companion, the beautiful Gisela, but was too shy to communicate his feelings to her. Ah, why had he left his native town? Furthermore it seemed that Jakob and Emmanuel had dreamed up the idea of having the young man settle in England, with a view toward a more lucrative profession and eventual marriage to Pauline, Emmanuel's daughter.

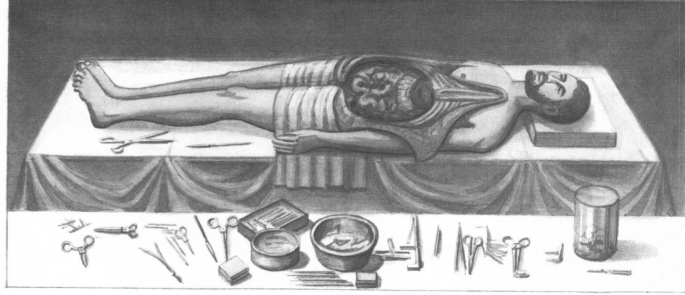

When he was nineteen he went to Manchester, but he was not at all attracted to the young girl. Unquestionably, this fact weighed heavily in his decision to take up a career in science.

At school he not only devoted almost thirty hours weekly to medical lectures and laboratory work, but also faithfully attended seminars in logic and philosophy.

Among his many courses, biology was his favorite. Ernst Brücke, professor of physiology and director of one of the laboratories, took notice of Freud and awarded him, among others, a scholarship for research at the Zoological Experimental Station at Trieste. Thus Freud became a true scholar. His subject of research: the gonadic structure of eels.

It is in vain that you range round from science to science; each man learns only what he can.

To the young researcher the work seemed fruitless and dull. Nevertheless, it was Freud's first contact, outside of books, with the Mediterranean civilization that was to play such an important role in his life and the elaboration of his ideas. Meanwhile, his intellectual enrichment was meager, with the exception perhaps of his awareness of the truth of Mephistopheles' conviction, whose words had for him a special meaning.

"At length in Ernst Brücke's Physiology Laboratory I found rest and satisfaction—and men, too, whom I could respect and take as my models: the great Brücke himself and his assistants Sigmund Exner and Ernst von Fleischl-Marxow, the eminent physician and physiologist" (*Autobiography*). Between 1877 and 1897, Freud published approximately twenty articles on neurology. Brücke remained for him an example of scientific probity; he was German (Austrians had the reputation of being less

disciplined) and the enemy of the pantheistic theorizing then in vogue. It was Brücke's influence that was responsible for Freud's profound belief in determinism. Freud was on the threshold of the neurone theory, but someone else would formulate it before him. After years of hard work in the laboratory, Freud decided to take his medical examination. He defined his predicament as a choice between "mutilating animals or tormenting human beings." The year was 1880.

The following year Freud obtained his medical degree, "owing to the clemency of fate or that of the examiners." The board of examiners was presided over by his friend Fleischl, and Freud came before that body trembling with fear. Despite his weakness in botany, the candidate received the grade of "excellent." As a child, Freud had had a photographic memory and "in the tension that preceded the final examination," Freud wrote years later, "I must have made use of the remnant of this ability, for in certain subjects I gave the examiners apparently automatic answers" (*Psychopathology of Everyday Life*).

Freud had mixed feelings about his choice of a career in medicine. In the few hours of free time his demanding studies allowed him, he turned to philosophy for escape and diversion. Thus he became familiar with the ideas of Plato, albeit indirectly, through his own excellent translations of John Stuart Mill.

Alas, my dear Freud, I can promise you no advancement in my department.

The difficult years during which Freud aspired to a teaching post in physiology were marked by serious financial troubles, and duty compelled him to abandon his academic hopes and take up the more lucrative practice of medicine. After all, one had to eat. But there was still a more pressing reason: Sigmund had fallen in love. How could he think of assuming the responsibilities of married life if he persisted in his selfish pursuit of an impecunious career as researcher? The young woman in question was Martha Bernays.

Details of Freud's life at the time are contained in his many letters to Martha. These letters are solemn and punctilious, but reveal an abundant literary talent. He had a decided preference for the colorful anecdote, providing it led to some tender or exalted sentiment, including, on occasion, even jealousy. In 1882, with a very modest salary, he took up his duties in medicine at the General Hospital of Vienna.

Underneath acute hallucinatory psychosis lies the mechanism of wish-fulfillment.

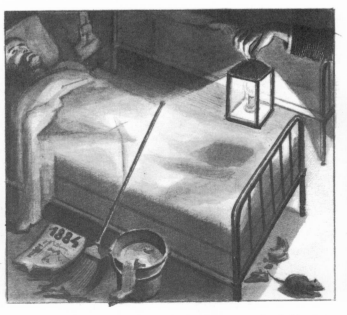

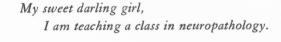

My sweet darling girl, I am teaching a class in neuropathology.

It was genuine inhibition that kept Freud from undivided commitment to his hospital work, so certain was he of failure: "My inadequate training does not admit of my practicing general medicine; I have learned what is needed to become a neurologist, nothing more." Freud soon became a resident in the psychiatric clinic under the directorship of Theodor Meynert, a well-known specialist in brain anatomy. He admired his chief but nevertheless had doubts concerning the talents of consulting doctors in the field of psychiatry; also, he was shocked by the archaic and unsanitary conditions of the wards. He aspired to the post of *Privatdozent*, a prestigious position that would permit him to give lectures on subjects outside the regular curriculum. Toward that end he began preparing a dossier by publishing case histories.

In 1885 Freud's ambition was fulfilled, thanks to Brücke's high praise of his work. How could the medical faculty refuse "a man with a good general education, of quiet and serious character, an excellent worker, of fine dexterity, clear vision, with the gift for well-organized written expression"?

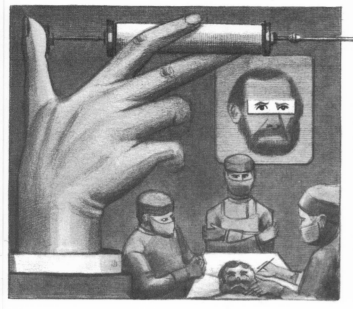

During this period, however, an unfortunate incident left a lasting scar on the medical researcher. Having been particularly impressed by the stimulating effects of cocaine, Freud viewed the drug as a remedy for various disorders, mental depression and morphine addiction among them. He enthusiastically recommended and prescribed cocaine to his friends as a euphoriant; and he used it, successfully and with pride, as an anesthetic in the correction of his father's glaucoma. He also encouraged its use for the relief of Fleischl's neuritic pain. With the first doses, massive and self-administered by injection, Fleischl felt much better and welcomed the drug as a substitute for his habitual morphine. But he was soon afflicted with delirium tremens. And one of Freud's patients died as a result of injudicious injections. Confronted by his colleagues' censure, Freud felt himself discredited.

The importance of these events was magnified in Freud's mind by his bitter self-reproach. His hurt was all the more painful because someone else's name became associated with the discovery of the analgesic qualities of cocaine. Despite his efforts to justify his actions, the ill-fated injections became a symbol of guilt in his later dreams.

The nearly one thousand letters Freud wrote to Martha provide many details of Freud's life during the years of his courtship. All was not serene. Moral questions, the milieu of their respective families, his financial difficulties only served to increase his impatience. At times he reproached his fiancée for her coolness, so removed from his own consuming passion. He became jealous of an artist friend who had once given her an innocent kiss. "I think there is general enmity," he wrote Martha, "between artists and those engaged in the details of scientific work. We know that they possess in their art a master key to open with ease all female hearts, whereas we stand helpless at the strange design of the lock and have first to torment ourselves to discover a suitable key to it." He even became jealous of Martha's family, insisting that her affection for her brother Eli and her mother was excessive. The long years of engagement seemed interminable.

Between 1882 and 1886, Freud's insecurity concerning Martha's love for him increased as her affection decreased. His self-doubts resulted in his testing her, awkwardly at times, or were transformed into galling fantasies, like the following: "We have just now such a heat wave as might be the cause of the most affectionate lovers parting. I picture the process thus. The girl is sitting in a corner as far as she can from the burning windows. He, whose love is even hotter than the thermometer, suddenly comes across to her and implants a warm kiss on her lips. She gets up, pushes him away, and cries out peevishly: 'Go away, I am too hot.' He stands there for a moment bewildered, and finally he turns round and leaves her. What she may be thinking is hidden from me, but I believe she rails at him and comes to the conclusion, 'If he is so petty as to feel hurt at that, he can't love me.'—That is what comes of the heat."

Perhaps even the desire to pursue a career in England, which reasserted itself forcefully soon after his engagement, had to do with the ambivalence of his feelings toward Martha. He could assert his independence from the one passion by devoting himself to another. In 1883 the Bernays family moved to the outskirts of Hamburg, and the few visits Freud made to that city only increased his feeling of solitude when he returned home.

Martha's occasional visits to the hospital where Freud had been an intern were now memories. In those days his life had become routine, but that was before the painful separation from Martha, when, despite his medical degree, he was plagued by countless problems and yearned for affective support. There were the demands of his teaching, the research that he was reluctant to give up, and his internship toward specialization; but he also had to face the fact of his father's growing impoverishment and the prospect of entering into marriage with almost no financial security.

Memories of visits from Martha. A single ray of sunshine finds its way into the poverty-stricken garret: the familiar romantic cliché? But consider also the sentimental moralizing of the young fiancé: "I will not conceal from you that some people declare you to be beautiful, even strikingly so. I have no opinion on the matter. Don't forget that 'beauty' only stays a few years, and that we have to spend a long life together. Once the smoothness and freshness of youth is gone then the only beauty lies where goodness and understanding transfigure the features." His romantic sentiments are further revealed in his choice of mottoes which Martha willingly embroidered in French for him to embellish the bare walls of the room where he spent long hours in study.

Also romantic, his preference in books: Dickens, who affected him greatly; Tasso's *Jerusalem Delivered*; and in another mode, Mark Twain's *Tom Sawyer*. But his favorite book was *Don Quixote*: "A great person, himself an idealist, makes fun of his ideals. We were all noble knights passing through the world caught in a dream, and cutting a sad figure. Therefore we men always read with respect about what we once were and in part still remain." Another favorite was Flaubert's *The Temptation of Saint Anthony*: "This book in the most condensed fashion and with unsurpassable vividness calls up not only the great problems of knowledge, but the real riddles of life, all the conflicts of feelings and impulses; and it confirms the awareness of our perplexity in the mysteriousness that reigns everywhere." And then the voice of the clinician: "The book is more readily understood with the realization that Flaubert was epileptic and himself subject to hallucinations."

Martha and Sigmund were married on September 14, 1886, in Germany. They had both agreed on the simplest of ceremonies. Freud had hoped that a civil marriage alone would suffice and was distressed to learn that without a religious ceremony their marriage would be invalid in Austria. Luckily for Freud the marriage took place on a weekday and very few people could attend. Following a honeymoon on the Baltic, the newlyweds settled in Vienna.

Without financial aid from friends they could never have dreamed of starting a life together. Among their benefactors were Fleischl; Freud's faithful friend Josef Breuer, whose influence would be so decisive; and Martha's aunt. Thus Dr. Freud began his private practice and anxiously awaited the arrival of patients. It was a propitious time, the final realization of his desires.

A significant gesture suggests that Freud may have seen married life as a new beginning. In a letter to Martha dated April 28, 1885, he wrote: "One intention I have almost finished carrying out, an intention which a number of as yet unborn and unfortunate people will resent: my biographers. I have destroyed all of my notes of the past fourteen years, as well as letters, scientific excerpts and manuscripts of my papers. As for letters, only those from

the family have been spared. Yours, my darling, were never in danger."

Money was necessary for marriage, and it was from love for his bride-to-be that Freud the neurologist spent the winter of 1885–86 studying with Jean Charcot at the Salpêtrière Clinic in Paris. The sum allotted for the traveling grant was considerable. Freud was assured of only

eight of the twenty-one votes to be cast for the competing candidates: "It is no good thinking of it. I must find some other way of winning you as my wife." The night before the final decision, Freud dreamed that Brücke had informed him he had no chance because there were seven rivals with better prospects. As might be expected, in the process of distortion common in dreams, Freud represented

Brücke as a beneficent force, the "protective father"; and was not he himself the preferred child over the other seven children in his own family? Finally, by a vote of thirteen to eight, he was awarded the grant: "I shall go to Paris and become a great *savant* and return to Vienna with a great, great nimbus. Then we will marry soon. . . . And they lived happily ever after."

Paris: How appropriate its Roman name, *Lutetia,* "the muddy town"! The "arrogant" French, with their difficult language, were "inaccessible." To make things worse it was the year of General Boulanger's rise to power. Already chauvinistic by nature, such Parisians as coachmen and shopkeepers, roused by the vengeful spirit of the "brav'

général," must not have viewed with favor the Germanic accent of the impecunious Austrian neurologist. And it was much the same at the hospital, where Charcot's disciples were quick to show their distrust of the foreigner. His visits to the Egyptian exhibits at the Louvre were small compensation for his enormous feeling of isolation, his

financial distress, and his separation from Martha. Fortunately he was befriended by Charcot, whose stature as a scientist made a lasting impression on the student. And his joy increased when the master entrusted him with the task of translating his works on neurology into German.

Only knowledge will give power.

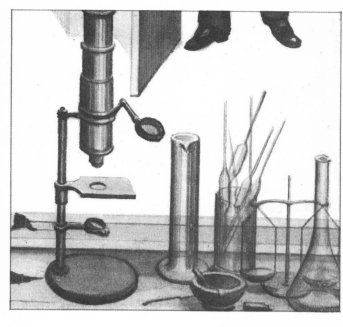

Freud's vision of the world at that time might be described as a synthesis of painfully contradictory scientific resolves counterbalanced by insistent intuitions he could not ignore without running the risk of giving up an important part of his being. It is tempting to review the old arguments of materialism, but it would be pointless: Freud cannot be confined within the oversimplifications of nineteenth-century positivism any more than he can be accused of undervaluing

empirical evidence in the formulation of his theories. Beginning in this period, however, he rejected simplistic classifications, as if already aware that the linking of phenomena occurred in some new and undiscovered arena. And in this respect he merits comparison with Plato, who enjoined us to leave appearances behind and come out of the cave where all is illusion. Also from Plato, he seemed to inherit the Greek reverence for the human gaze: it was

not for nothing that the blind Oedipus would come to represent for Freud the model of human fate.

But the comparison with Plato ends there. The field of the microscope is necessarily limited; not that the *real* cannot be thoroughly examined there, but *reality* is not there made manifest. As Freud already knew, symbols are an integral part of reality, if indeed the symbolism of mental activity includes the manner in which the subject

juggles reality with his choice of words. Although Freud was not yet aware of the importance of his discovery, he suspected its validity. He also surmised that what people said, their "proposals," were actually enticing "propositions"; this example of truth distortion he would test on himself.

> *Only knowledge will give power.*

The fact is that Freud had arrived at a significant juncture. Among his many published articles on neurology, he gave preference to those dealing with the problems of aphasia, thus revealing the importance he attached to the spoken word. Since speech originates in the brain, its function "signifies" that organ both as mind and as body. Although influenced by contemporary thought which denied perception

any priority over the thing perceived, Freud nevertheless expressed an original view when he proposed the existence of "unconscious psychical processes which are a part of the complex framework of mental activity and which require no active participation of the brain." Still, the impression remains that these bits of theory, like so many stumbling blocks, in no way point to the qualitative leaps yet to come

in Freud's thinking. If his theoretical work had remained within the field of neurology, his efforts would have no more than historical interest. But he was delivered from this purely academic fate by his decision to begin a circumscribed exploration within himself. Like Montaigne, he reasoned there was no surer way to an understanding of the human condition than to "essay himself."

Much of the psychism is formed by layers from the past;

and the present is only tangential to this earlier stratification. A way had to be found within the labyrinth of this ancient city, but the sacrifice of immediate interests is its price.

Also, that other tetragram formed by the word *papa* had to be carefully examined, including the traces left on the son by the mighty Jakob. With uncertainty Freud focused his attention on the point where the demands of the species

converge with the individual's need for autonomy. He was not able to consider the problem clearly until, in the course of his "archeological digging," he was made to contemplate the deep layers of the mind. And the promise of uncovering the remains of ancient structures was offered in the form of another implement for investigation, more efficient than the eye. This new tool was called listening.

In 1887 Freud began using hypnotism in his private practice, which consisted mainly of neurotic patients. He remembered as a student having been vividly impressed while witnessing a hypnotist at work; and he had seen the procedure used on occasion in his recent work with Charcot in Paris. Nervous disorders at the time were routinely treated by the use of baths or electricity, but with little success. It was thus that Freud turned to hypnosis, enjoying thereby a certain prestige among his bourgeois patients, who saw him as a sort of miracle worker, unafraid to experiment with new and original methods. But not everyone was pleased: the Viennese medical establishment became aroused, angered even, by this "charlatan."

He was well aware that his former chief Meynert, motivated more by personal than scientific reasons, used the occasion to try to discredit him. Yet Freud failed to take into account one important factor in his method of treatment—the role of the patient eager to please the doctor. In his own defense Freud asserted that not only did he improve the well-being of patients, but he was able to uncover the original traumatic event that provoked the illness:

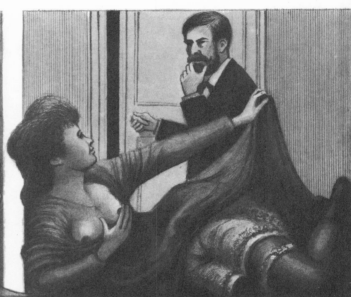

Emmy von N., for example, had a fear of toads because in childhood her brother in play had tormented her with one of these creatures. And still another success: during two treatments under hypnosis a young woman was cured of her inability to nurse her own child because of obstructing hysterical symptoms, such as vomiting. Freud recognized that in cases of hysteria the subject's will to carry out an intention is thwarted by his unawareness of combatting forces that gain the upper hand in moments of exhaustion or excitement. But because of his limited knowledge of psychical conflict, he did not inquire into the nature of these inhibitions. Along with his victories in hypnosis, there were defeats; but even these proved fruitful in the development of his theory. He learned, for example, that the patient's erotic relationship with the doctor is an almost inevitable part of the cure, though usually manifested in a more discreet fashion than the unequivocal invitation offered him by one female patient. Recognizing the value of the subject's attraction to the doctor, he decided to give up the mask of hypnosis, which merely encouraged the skirting of reality, and concentrate on the phenomenon of *transference*.

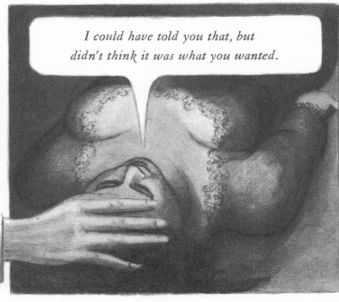

There was the case of Elisabeth, who was refractory to hypnosis. Freud asked her to concentrate on one of her symptoms and try to tell him anything that would throw light on its cause. If nothing happened, the doctor pressed her forehead with his hand and assured her she would eventually find the answer. It was then that Freud discovered the meaning of *censorship*, which caused the patient to reject as unworthy ideas that seemed removed from the problem at hand. But it was these seemingly unrelated observations that shed the most light on the patient's emotional conflict. The new discovery soon led Freud to give up asking questions and to encourage his patients to freely voice their most intimate thoughts in unordered spontaneity.

From the listening sessions emerged the startling fact that each patient revealed some dark bedroom secret, or the memory of an unpleasant sexual experience at a very early age. Unwilling at first to draw conclusions from the evidence, he did however recall the prescription of a distinguished Viennese gynecologist who had sent him a female patient: "Repeated doses of a normal penis." An impotent husband was the cause of her severe anxiety.

Freud's new knowledge eventually led to a breach between him and his faithful and generous friend Breuer. It was this eminent physiologist, Freud's senior by fourteen years, who in 1882 had given him details of a case history decisive to the future of psychoanalysis. After his return from Paris, Freud took renewed interest in Breuer's effective treatment of Anna O.'s hysteria. Under hypnosis the patient would recount traumatic events leading to her illness, and, with the surfacing of what was suppressed during her waking state, symptoms would disappear. In 1895, at Freud's insistence, the case of Anna O. was included in *Studies on Hysteria*, published jointly by the two men. There arose, however, deep disagreement between the coauthors: according to Breuer, Anna seemed to be "an asexual being," and he was not inclined to accept Freud's sexual etiology of neurosis. To be sure, Breuer stood behind his associate when confronted by their medical colleagues, but he remained unconvinced; and Freud finally ended their relationship, thereby committing the first of his symbolic "patricides." Also, he had been corresponding for several years with Wilhelm Fliess, a man for whom he had much esteem and who, Freud reasoned, would better understand his ideas.

It is customary to trace the beginning of psychoanalysis to the case of Anna O., which had a curious conclusion. Breuer's wife became extremely jealous of her husband's attentions to his patient, and as a gesture toward conjugal harmony, treatment was ended. Anna, however, imagining herself pregnant from Breuer's ministrations, experienced a hysterical childbirth. Soon after, Breuer and his wife vacationed in Venice, where they conceived a child of their own.

Unquestionably, Freud's path was opened in part by Charcot, whose *Nouvelles leçons* and *Leçons du mardi* Freud had translated into German when he returned from Paris. From this experience with Charcot, Freud was alerted to the essentially psychological nature of the treatment of hysteria, even though the procedure lacked any neurologic basis: "Many of Charcot's demonstrations," Freud would later write, "began by provoking in me and in other visitors a sense of astonishment and an inclination to skepticism, which we tried to justify by an appeal to one of the theories of the day. He was always friendly and patient in dealing with such doubts, but he was also most decided; it was in one of these discussions that he remarked, '*Ça n'empêche pas d'exister*,' a *mot* which left an indelible mark upon my mind."

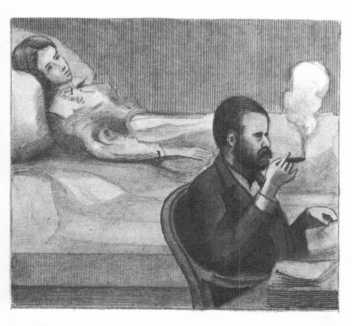

Freud's exploratory technique was modified to exclude the psychotherapist's active intervention in his relation with the patient. He no longer sought to hypnotize, to suggest, or to encourage the flow of words. His only requirement was the reclining position, which seemed to facilitate the free association of ideas and diminish reticence. Later, he would sit behind the patient so as to interfere even less.

With its theoretic potential, *Studies on Hysteria* was a landmark, despite its cool reception in medical circles. But it was given to poet Alfred von Bergner to signal the dawning of the new revolution: "We dimly conceive the idea that it may one day become possible to approach the innermost secret of human personality. . . . The theory itself is in fact nothing but the kind of psychology used by poets."

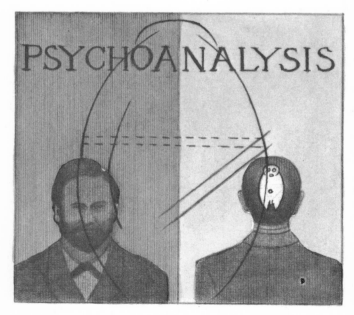

Freud had replaced Brücke first with Charcot and then with Breuer. It was now time for him to spread his own wings, taking the metaphor used by Breuer himself, who said: "Freud's intellect is soaring at its highest. I gaze after him as a hen at a hawk."

In 1896, for the first time, an article in French used the word *psychoanalysis*.

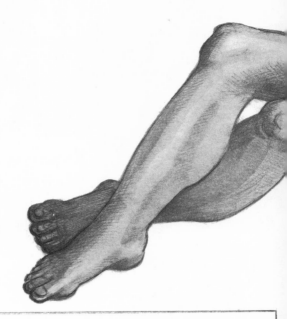

Let us suppose a system φ which transmits the perception of an external object χ to consciousness. The machine is so regulated that ψ, the unconscious, gathers up information in neurones, certain of which, owing to a network of "contact-barriers," allow a given quantity of excitation to arrive in consciousness as memory; others, conversely, set up obstacles along this route. A third system of neurones, ω, which is excited along with perception, informs the organism of the objective reality of the perceived object and links the subject's present experience to memory-traces set down in ψ. Such was Freud's description of the psychical apparatus in his "Project for a Scientific Psychology" (1895), which unquestionably bore the stamp of a quantitative theory. Naïve, it nevertheless foreshadowed the problems involved in the formulation of the *ego*.

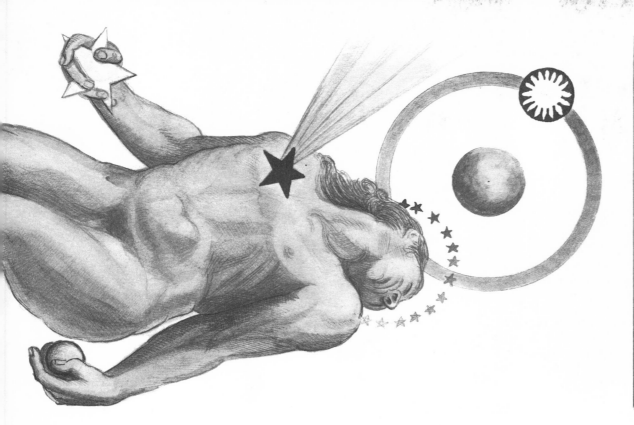

For this psychology Freud was indebted to others of the nineteenth century, most of them nearly forgotten today. Johann Herbart, for example, had envisioned a "mathematical psychology," stressing the parallel between the regular order in the human mind and that of the "starry sky," where the less brilliant stars represent what is censored, and those eclipsed the indirect effects of stirrings "behind the curtains" of consciousness. And there was Gustave Fechner, who systematized the concept of *threshold* and likened the mind to a floating iceberg whose course is determined not only by the surface winds but also by the unknown currents of the deep.

But Freud's originality lies elsewhere: first, because he went beyond this mechanistic view and introduced the idea of the pleasure-unpleasure principle, which involves the subject in making choices; second, because he insisted on the mechanism of repression or exclusion from consciousness, in part voluntary. He transformed the purely quantitative value of this psychology by associating it with the notion of pleasure resulting from the discharge of tension. The protective shield against excessive stimuli is part of the natural economy of the system. Finally, Freud introduced the idea that what is driven from consciousness is *always* sexual in origin.

In a dream he had had thirty years earlier, Freud
recognized the traces of sexual trauma in childhood:
he dreamed he saw his mother "with a peaceful, sleeping expression
on her features, being carried into the room by two (or three)
people with kinds of beaks and laid upon the bed."

"A scene occurred to me which, for the last twenty-nine years, has occasionally emerged in my conscious memory without my understanding it. My mother was nowhere to be found: I was screaming my head off. My brother Philipp was holding open a box for me, and, when I found that my mother was not inside it either, I began crying still more, till, looking slim and beautiful, she came in by the door."

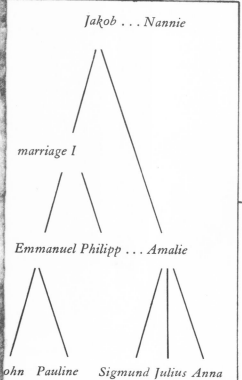

Jakob . . . Nannie

marriage I

Emmanuel Philipp . . . Amalie

ohn Pauline Sigmund Julius Anna

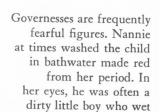

His father's second marriage had complicated the family structure, and for many years Sigmund was unable to understand the age relationship of successive generations. His brother Philipp, for example, was twenty years older than he.

Governesses are frequently fearful figures. Nannie at times washed the child in bathwater made red from her period. In her eyes, he was often a dirty little boy who wet himself, and a good-for-nothing imbecile. On occasion she called him "muttonhead." But Goethe himself, one of Freud's heroes, had studied the bone structure of the head of sheep. . . .

At the age of forty, Freud was given an icy reception when he addressed his colleagues in Vienna on the subject of the sexual origin of neuroses. It was then he decided to break from the medical society of learned men.

Freud's opposition to accepted ideas made his position uneasy. His medical confreres in Vienna considered his undue attention to the problems of hysteria a pursuit unworthy of a true doctor; and he was the object of still further hostility resulting from a growing ostracism of Jewish practitioners.

Added to these worries was a concern about his private practice. As a faithful disciple of Charcot, he was certain that neurologic disturbances could be treated by an IDEA alone; and he also knew that this idea revolved around the sexual life of the patient.

In a dream in July 1895, answers to questions concerning Freud's personal ambitions and public pronouncements of theory were revealed in condensed form in the guise of statements that were both demand and plea:

Why didn't you accept my solution? If you still get pains, it's really your own fault.

If you only knew what pains I have. They're choking me.

Have I been overlooking some organic trouble all along?

"A large hall—numerous guests, whom we were receiving.

Among them was Irma.

I at once took her to one side . . ."

She refuses
to open her mouth;
it's as if she had
false teeth.

It's an infection!
But dysentery will
eliminate the toxin.

TRIMETHYLAMINE

"It's not my fault if patients don't get well,
Irma no less than the rest.

"If only they would
open their mouths and talk,
things would go much
better.

"Also, things would be better if
only the lover were more
disposed to using his . . .
syringe.

"Scientists, loyal friends,
common sense even, will prove that
I am right in my sexual etiology
of neurosis.

"As for my wife's pregnancy
(and no one but myself is responsible
for that),

"I must go on hoping
I have not endangered her health.

"No!
I am fully accountable
for that life which is yet to come:
Anna will be born!

"Just as a new science will be born,
of which I can rightly boast that
I am its father:

the theory of the unconscious."

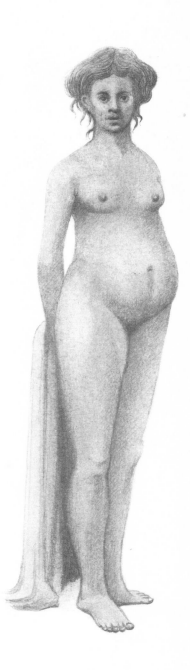

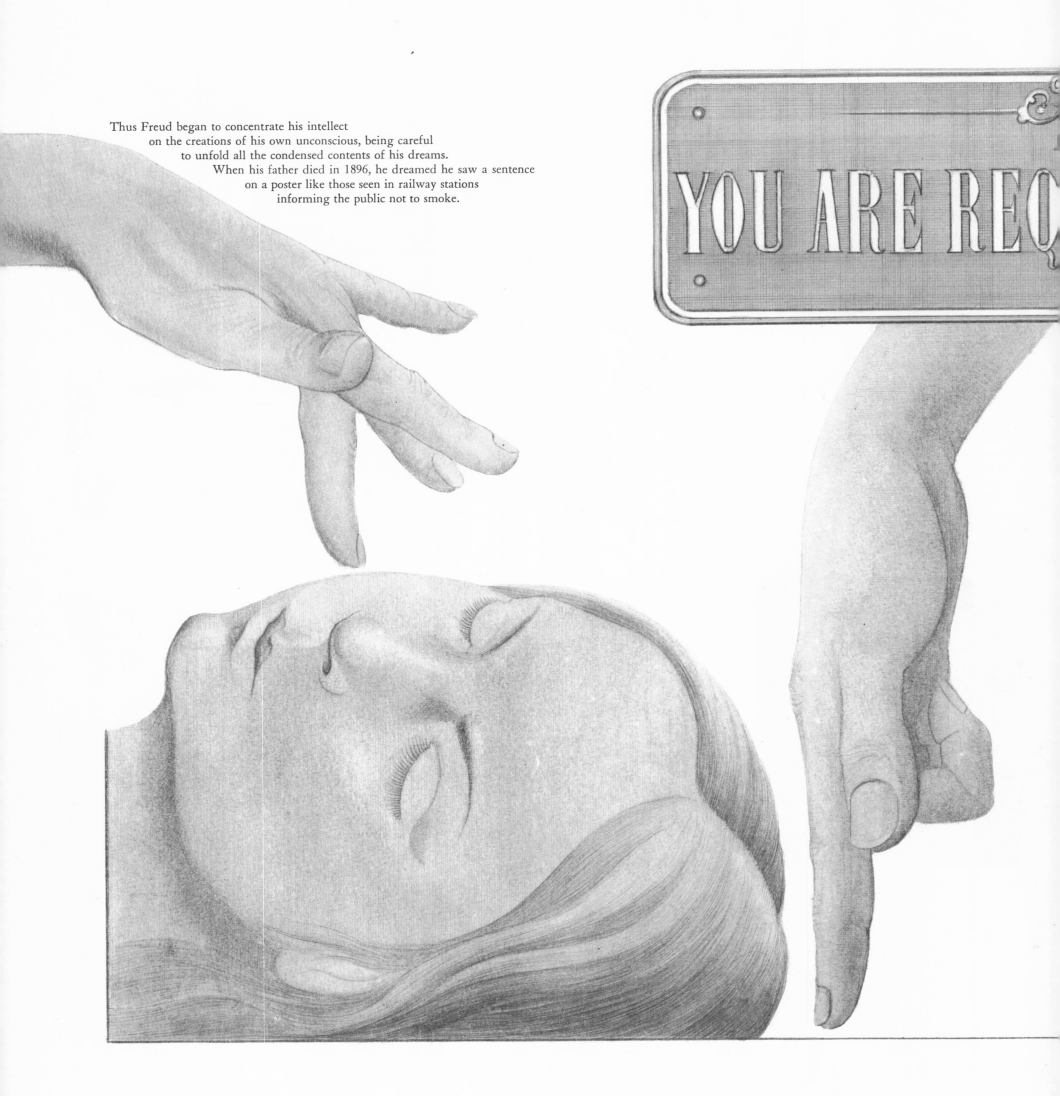

Thus Freud began to concentrate his intellect
on the creations of his own unconscious, being careful
to unfold all the condensed contents of his dreams.
When his father died in 1896, he dreamed he saw a sentence
on a poster like those seen in railway stations
informing the public not to smoke.

YOU ARE REQ

CLOSE YOUR EYES

REFRAIN FROM SMOKING

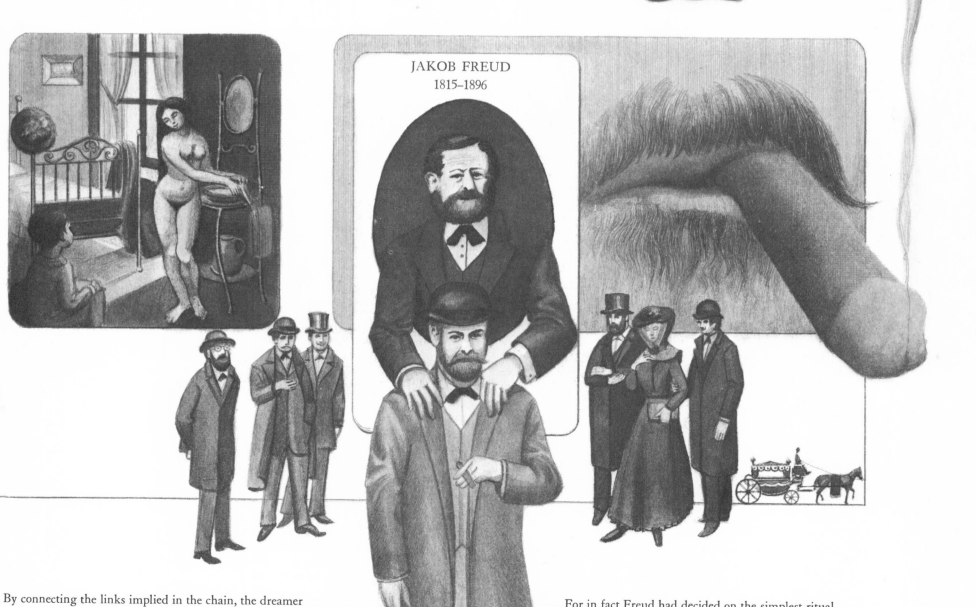

UESTED TO

Freud admitted to one phobia: he hated trains. During a trip he took with his mother from Leipzig to Vienna, when he was four years old, he had his first remembered erotic experience in the hotel room he shared with her. In 1894, when he was thirty-eight, concern for his health made him quit smoking his habitual cigars; but his efforts to control his habit merely resulted in a state of general depression.

JAKOB FREUD
1815–1896

By connecting the links implied in the chain, the dreamer understood the wish-fulfillment that lay behind the dream: he was seeking indulgence for his disregard of the ancient customs of burial; people were requested to close their eyes to the scandal.

For in fact Freud had decided on the simplest ritual possible for his father's funeral. Also, he was begging the dead man's forgiveness for his negligence—and for many other things as well.

WORKING IN ISOLATION, FREUD
CARRIES ON HIS CRUSADE AGAINST MEDICAL
AUTHORITY BY LEANING ON HIS ALTER EGO.

Wilhelm Fliess was an otolaryngologist from Berlin, two years younger than Sigmund. He was a brilliant specialist given to abstract thought, whom Freud hoped might furnish the precise anatomical data he needed to encourage him in his struggles. The two doctors had in common their Jewish middle-class origin, similar scientific interests, and mutual esteem. From this there developed a truly passionate attachment.

If this "love affair," or transference, as it would later be called, elicits an indulgent smile, it is well not to overlook the important role played by Fliess in heightening Freud's genuine analytic awareness. Although many of Fliess's contributions were no more than naïve intuitions, they were given the benefit of every doubt; and what remained of them when the theory of the unconscious was finally developed had been carefully tested by Freud against the tenets of science.

Although the field of medicine was their common meeting ground, the two physicians aspired to go beyond the limits of science. In a letter to his friend, Freud wrote: "I see that you are reaching, by the circuitous path of medicine, your first ideal, that of understanding human beings as a physiologist, just as I cherish the hope of arriving, by the same route, at my original goal of philosophy. For that was my earliest aim, when I did not know what I was in the world for."

Still, Fliess's mystical convictions could not stand up under scientific scrutiny. His pronouncements, readily accepted by Freud and somehow incorporated into his own thinking, had the single merit of proceeding from the then very unpopular idea that "sexual problems are at the root of pathology."

Dysmenorrhea is nasal in origin.

There is no longer any doubt about the sexual symbolism of the nose.

All human beings are bisexual. The number 28 refers to the feminine component, 23 to the masculine one.

Homosexuality is an important part of the psychism.

Sexual periods, in men and women alike, explain the phenomena of life and death.

The unconscious cannot be explained without taking into account the tendency to repeat behavior.

August 1, 1890

Dear Fliess, . . . I am writing to you today to tell you, very much against the grain, that I cannot come to Berlin; not that I care about Berlin or the Congress, but I am so disappointed that I shall not be able to see you there. . . . I do so most unwillingly, because I expected a great deal from meeting you. Though otherwise quite satisfied, happy if you like, I feel very isolated, scientifically blunted, stagnant and resigned. When I talked to you, and saw that you thought something of me, I actually started thinking something of myself, and the picture of confident energy which you offered was not without its effect. . . .
Your devoted Sigm. Freud

October 20, 1895

Dear Wilhelm, . . . If I had waited a fortnight before setting it [the "Project"] all down for you it would have been so much clearer. But it was only in the process of setting it down that I cleared it up for myself. So it could not be helped. . . . If I could talk to you about nothing else for forty-eight hours on end the thing could probably be finished. . . . You will not have any objection to my calling my next son Wilhelm! If *he* turns out to be a daughter, *she* will be called Anna. With cordial greetings, Your Sigm.

December 8, 1895

Dear Wilhelm, . . . As for your discoveries in sexual physiology, I can only promise close attention and critical admiration. My knowledge is too limited for me to be able to intervene. But I look forward to fine and important things, and I hope that when the time comes you will not fail to come out in the open even with hypotheses. We cannot do without men with the courage to think new things before they can prove them. Many things would be different if we were not geographically separated. . . . Cordial greetings from all here to wife and daughter. Your Sigm.

April 28, 1897

My dear Wilhelm, . . . I had a dream last night which concerned you. . . . I wanted you for my audience, to tell you about some of my ideas and the outcome of my recent work. . . . I felt a sense of irritation with you, as if you were claiming something special for yourself. . . . As I am still doubtful myself about matters concerned with the father-figure, my touchiness is intelligible. The dream thus collected all the irritation with you that was present in my unconscious. . . .

May 16, 1897

My dear Wilhelm, . . . I hope you will now remain your old self for a good long time and allow me to go on taking advantage of your good nature as an indulgent audience. . . .

May 31, 1897

My dear Wilhelm, . . . Herewith a few fragments I have jotted down for your eyes alone. . . . Another presentiment tells me that I am about to discover the source of morality. . . . If only you were nearer, so that I could tell you about it more easily. . . .
Your Sigm.

July 7, 1897

My dear Wilhelm, . . . Something from the deepest depths of my own neurosis has ranged itself against my taking a further step in understanding of the neuroses, and you have somehow been involved. My inability to write seems to be aimed at hindering our intercourse. . . .Your Sigm.

October 15, 1897

My dear Wilhelm, . . . My interest has been so exclusively concentrated on the analysis that I have not yet set about trying to answer the question whether, instead of my hypothesis that repression always proceeds from the female side and is directed against the male, the converse may hold good, as you suggested. Unfortunately I can contribute so little to your work and progress. In one respect I am better off than you. What I have to say about the mental side of this world finds in you an understanding critic; what you tell me about its starry side rouses in me only barren admiration. Your Sigm.

January 30, 1899

My dear Wilhelm, . . . You can have no idea how much your visit raised my spirits. I am still living on it. The light has not gone out since; little bits of new knowledge glimmer now here, now there, which is truly refreshing after the comfortlessness of last year. . . . But I have nothing big and complete yet. I am diligently making notes of the significant features, to lay before you at the Congress. I need you as my audience. Your Sigm.

March 23, 1900

My dear Wilhelm, . . . There has never been a period in which the wish that we lived in the same place as you and your family has affected me so deeply and constantly as in the past six months. You know I have been going through a deep inner crisis, and if we meet you would see how it has aged me. So I was deeply touched when I was told of your proposal that we should meet at Easter. Anyone who did not understand the more subtle resolution of contradictions would think it incomprehensible that I am not hastening to assent to the proposal. In point of fact it is more probable that I shall avoid you—not only because of my almost childish yearning for the spring and the beauties of nature, which I would willingly sacrifice for the pleasure of your company for three days. But there are other, inner reasons, an accumulation of imponderables, which weigh heavily on me. . . . Your devoted Sigm.

February 15, 1901

My dear Wilhelm, . . . I shall no more get to Rome this Easter than you will. What you say has explained to me the meaning of what would otherwise have remained an unintelligible interpolation in my last letter. Behind it there was, of course, a reference to the promise you once gave me in happier times, to hold a Congress with me on classical soil. I was only escaping from the present into the most beautiful of my former fantasies. . . . Meanwhile the Congresses themselves have become relics of the past; I am doing nothing new, and, as you say, I have become entirely estranged from what you are doing.

August 7, 1901

My dear Wilhelm, . . . There is no concealing the fact that we have drawn somewhat apart from each other. . . . You take sides against me and tell me that "the thought-reader merely reads his own thoughts into other people" . . . [The Psychopathology of Everyday Life] . . . is full of references to you: obvious ones, where you supplied the material, and concealed ones, where the motivation derives from you. Apart from any permanent value that its contents may have, you can take it as a testimonial to the role you have hitherto played in my life. . . . Your Sigm.

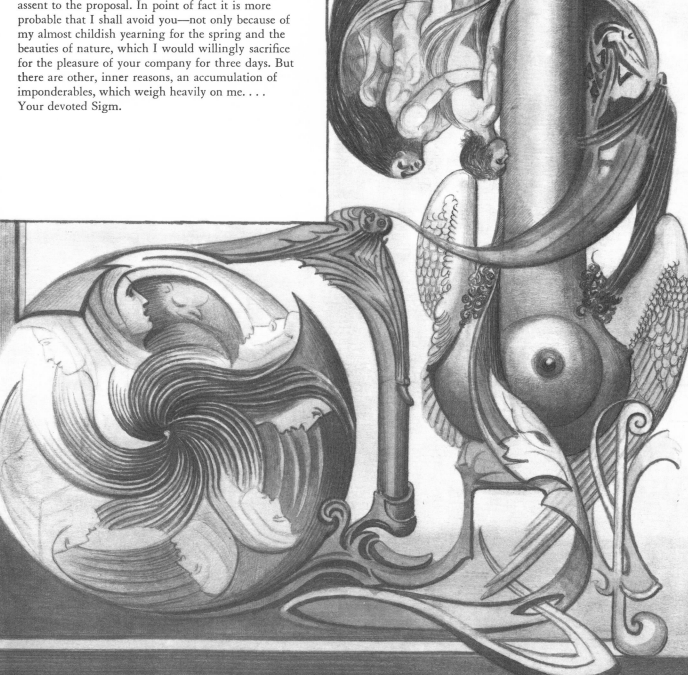

Whenever they had a few free days the two dedicated researchists held a "Congress" where each in turn was audience to the other. They held their meetings in various places: Berlin, Vienna sometimes, but also Salzburg, Munich, Breslau, or in quiet country towns in the Tyrol. The idea of meeting in Rome often came up, but was never fulfilled.

Vienna, January 3, 1899

I live gloomily and in darkness until you come, and then I pour out all my grumbles to you, kindle my flickering light at your steady flame and feel well again; and after your departure I have eyes to see again, and what I look upon is good. Sigm.

If Freud avoided his friend's proposed rendezvous for Easter 1900 in Rome, it was because that city was charged with symbolic meaning. Just as the Semite Hannibal had promised his father to avenge him for the affront the Romans inflicted upon him, so Freud had long been outraged by the memory of an incident Jakob recounted when Sigmund was a boy concerning the humiliation he once suffered from a gentile. So long as he remained under the influence of Fliess, Freud relived with intensity his affective feelings relating to the idea of "father."

Besides, the desire to visit Rome, nurtured during the period of their passionate friendship, had become meaningless by 1900, for the two men had already become strangers. The Congress did not materialize, and when Freud finally went to Rome he was accompanied by his brother Alexander. The prolonged adolescence of his attachment to Fliess was over.

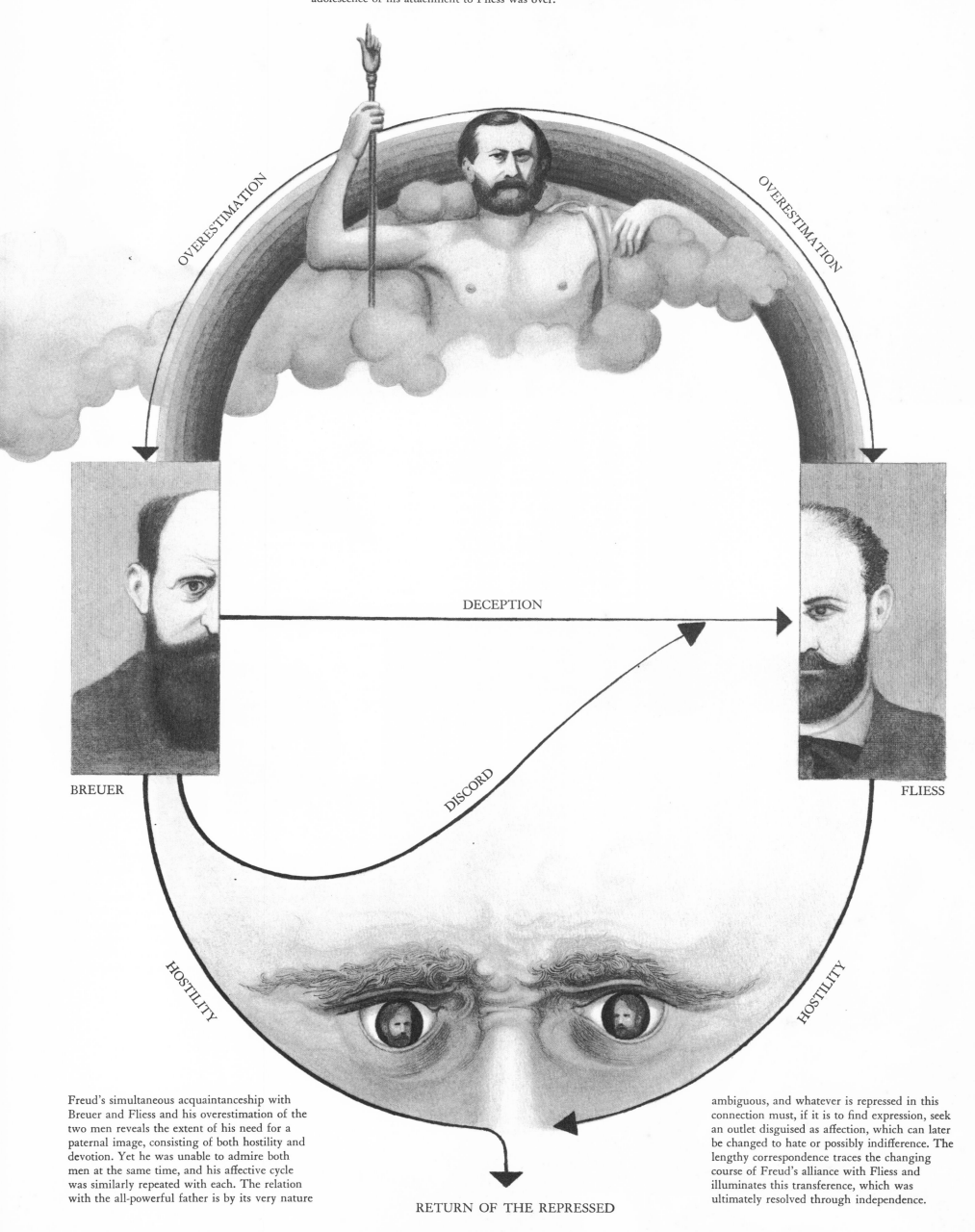

OVERESTIMATION

OVERESTIMATION

DECEPTION

BREUER

FLIESS

DISCORD

HOSTILITY

HOSTILITY

Freud's simultaneous acquaintanceship with Breuer and Fliess and his overestimation of the two men reveals the extent of his need for a paternal image, consisting of both hostility and devotion. Yet he was unable to admire both men at the same time, and his affective cycle was similarly repeated with each. The relation with the all-powerful father is by its very nature

ambiguous, and whatever is repressed in this connection must, if it is to find expression, seek an outlet disguised as affection, which can later be changed to hate or possibly indifference. The lengthy correspondence traces the changing course of Freud's alliance with Fliess and illuminates this transference, which was ultimately resolved through independence.

RETURN OF THE REPRESSED

Freud's self-analysis did not fundamentally contradict the principles set forth in the "Project" of 1895. Dreams are the hallucinatory fulfillment of primordial wishes presented in a rudimentary yet organized sequence of images. Freud described a dream in which a woman intimately put her hand on his knee, telling him, "You've always had such beautiful eyes." The analysis of the dream revealed an intricate association of impulses and affects relating to avarice and debt which were closely bound up with the notion of "eyes." Often a dream revolves around a partial image—a look, a mouth, a breast—and allows us to reexperience a deeply repressed situation. Yet in waking states things are much the same in the process of reality-testing: desire is the single motivating force of the psychical apparatus. Thus the baby cries to satisfy its hunger, and its mother hastens to feed it. To prevent the remembrance of satisfaction from finding fulfillment in hallucination, it is necessary for consciousness—and this is its essential role when functioning properly—to inhibit memory so that it does not become perception. It is this same process which causes us to shun a memory-image associated with displeasure: the perceptual system partially abandons the repressed mnemic image in favor of rational thought.

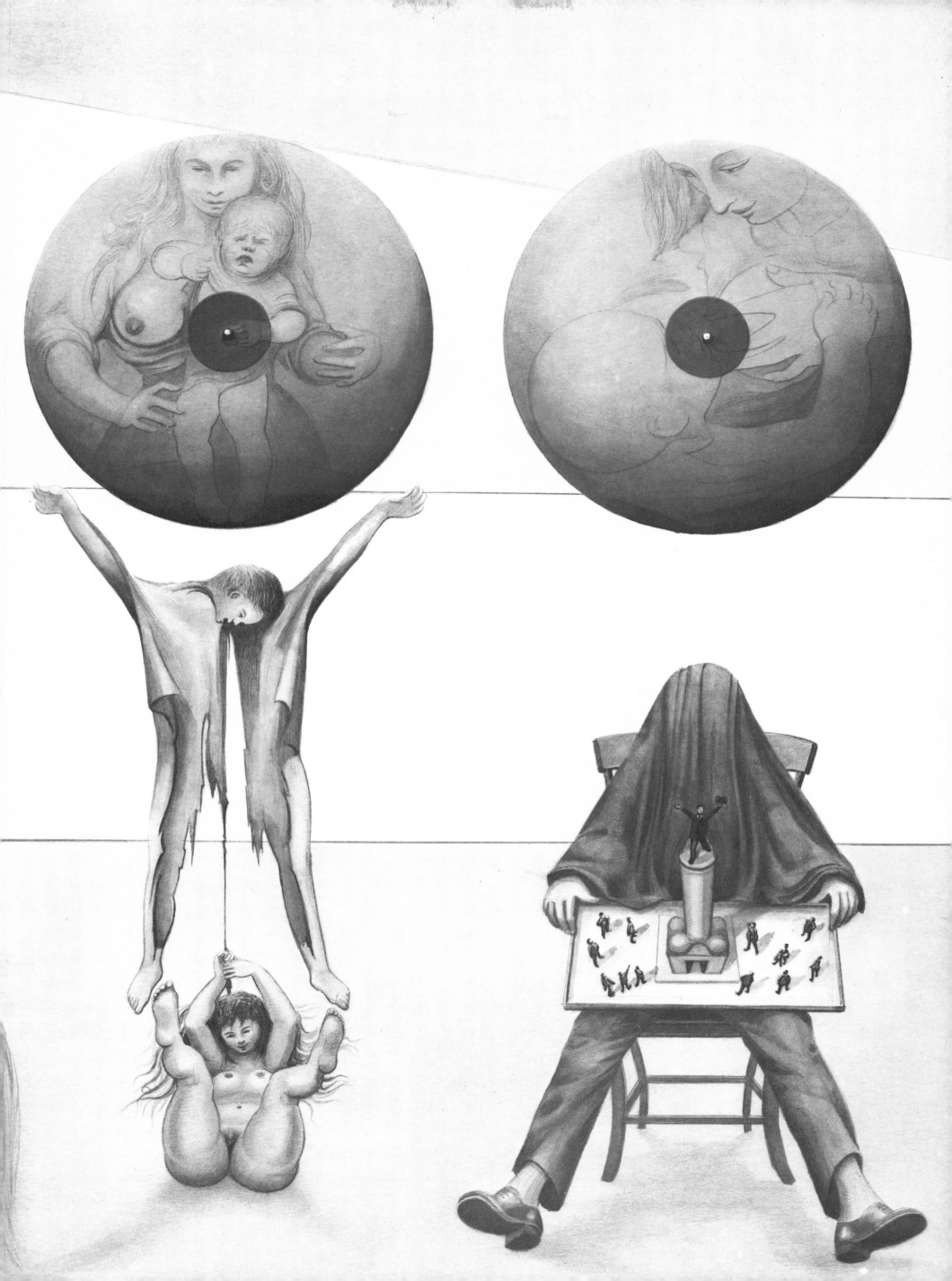

In his *Psychopathology of Everyday Life*, Freud gave scientific status to the mechanism of forgetfulness, asserting that forgetting names and words is not merely a lapse, but constitutes a revealing language in itself.

While on a trip through Herzegovina, Freud discussed with his fellow passenger, a cultivated stranger, the customs of the Turks living in the region. Their conversation then turned to Italy and painting, and in particular the frescoes in the cathedral at Orvieto, executed by Signorelli, a name quite familiar to Freud but which he could not remember at the time. Two substitute names came to mind: Botticelli then Boltraffio; but he was unable to recall the right name until he asked someone at a later time. As soon as he heard the correct surname, he remembered the painter's given name, Luca, and realized that "repression was at work and not true forgetfulness." Indeed, investigation revealed that the repression was tied up with ideas of death and sexuality.

An abyss of intricate thoughts opened up when Freud began to analyze the memory lapse. The most obvious centered on the repressed syllables SIGNOR, the Italian equivalent of the German *Herr* (Sir), arrived at by the removal of ELLI, common to both Botticelli and Signorelli. One could easily conjecture that the religious subject of the fresco in question, the *Last Judgment*, was not without significance, since *Elli* means "my God" in Hebrew, a language Freud had studied as a boy and which his father spoke and wrote.

Trafoi

Bo-*ttic*ELLI

Bo-*l-Traffio*

Turks

Bo-*snia*

Sir

HER-*zegovina*

SIGNOR-ELLI

Also, Freud had learned from one of his colleagues that the Turks submit passively to the death of a loved one, without ever incriminating the attending physician. (BOtticelli and BOltraffio are suggested by BOsnia, which in turn is associated with HERzegovina and the Turks.) So much for death, the central theme of the *Last Judgment*, which also depicts the sadistic tortures of hell by combining medieval obsessions and sexualized robust bodies in the manner that would later characterize the work of Michelangelo. The latter was of importance to Freud not just for intellectual reasons (his *Moses* fascinated him), but because of the association with Fliess and their planned trip to Rome. In fact, some time earlier Freud had forgotten the name of the German poet Julius Mosen (whose "Moses" indirectly attacks Pope Julius II). Amalie Freud's second son, who died at the age of eight months, was named Julius, and as a child Sigmund would have willingly seen him in hell, just as later he would have gladly sent Fliess to the devil. For Freud had learned about hell from his "pious" Nannie, who probably threatened him with damnation if he committed the "solitary sin." And so we are led back to the theme of sexuality and once more to the Turks, for whom apparently sensual pleasure is a necessity of life, a fact they

readily confide to their doctors, but which Freud took care not to communicate to his fellow passenger, a Berlin lawyer named Freyhau. This name itself is not without significance: *frei*, meaning free (suggesting freedom from all restraints, including the interdict against love of mother), and its last syllable, the city of Breslau, where Freud had an unpleasant Congress with Fliess. It was at Breslau also, during the trip to Leipzig when Freud was three years old, that from the train window he saw flaming gas jets which made him think of souls burning in hell; and a subsequent trip the following year was the occasion for sharing a hotel room with his mother and seeing her naked. Thus the old Oedipal leaning seemed to be revived in the mechanism of forgetfulness. Consider also the association with the name *Luca Signorelli*: the first three letters of Freud's given name are identical to the first three of the painter's surname. In memory of his dead grandfather Schlomo, Freud was originally named Sigismund, which he shortened to Sigmund, "conqueror by the mouth" (at the breast? by the word?). By ridding his name of the extra syllable he renounced his filiation both with the grandfather and with his father, Jakob, also called ISrael.

Thus the hostility toward his father was concealed by a dual disavowal, or more precisely by a fixation on his grandfather (as well as on his brother Julius), and by his repudiation of the ancestral rabbinical tradition in favor of universal light, LUX (Luca, Lucifer). For what is psychoanalysis but the shedding of light in the darkest of corners? And the theory was hardly born when its "father" a few weeks earlier at *Trafoi* received disquieting news concerning one of his patients with an incurable sexual disorder: carrying the Turks' reasoning to its logical conclusion, the man committed suicide. Understandably, Freud made no mention of this to Freyhau; or, more accurately, he communicated it fleetingly under the guise of the name *Boltraffio*, which was a compromise between silence and avowal. All these anxieties assume their full meaning within the context of guilt feelings associated with Freud's need to excel in science. Years later, commenting on his work, Freud wrote: "It is as though the most important thing in success is to go beyond one's father, while at the same time it is forbidden to surpass him." And for that matter, *Signor* is just another way of saying *Senior*, the elder.

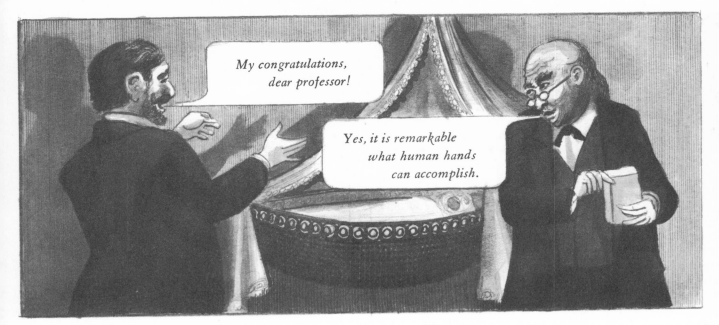

Freud's theories concerning mistakes in speech and action found confirmation in still another area of psychical activity which also deals with language and communication: the world of jokes. Jokes exist, of course, for pleasure; but they frequently revolve around innuendo, and for an interpreter such as Freud they were readily associated with the mechanism of censorship. And it must be noted that Freud himself had his own repertoire of jokes, Jewish jokes, in which the meaning behind the comic effect was usually accompanied by an inherent ambiguity. For in fact the jokes made by Jews about themselves include the enumeration of their own intrinsic weaknesses, and are therefore marked by endless anti-Semitism. By communicating these self-deprecating jokes, Jews openly admit their foibles and seem to anticipate and disarm the aggression to which they are constantly subjected.

Certainly, the anecdotes recounted by Freud in *Jokes and their Relation to the Unconscious* (1905) are not all Jewish, but their prevailing tone is clearly associated with ghetto humor. Not necessarily Jewish, for example, is the dignified professor who alludes to his advanced age by replying equivocally to the compliment paid him on the birth of his youngest child. Freud's concern in the book is always with *meaning*, and the frequent references to Jews

are a convenient way of stressing the connection between the subject and his mode of expression. There is for instance the portmanteau word coined by the indigent lottery agent who combines two ideas into one, as in dreams, by boasting that the Baron Rothschild treated him quite "famillionairely"; and the sophistry of the man who borrowed a kettle, answering the complaining lender that first of all he never borrowed a kettle; that secondly, the

kettle had a hole in it when he got it; and that thirdly, he gave it back undamaged. Such illustrations would satisfy the pathologist of language or of thought processes, but Freud the psychoanalyst went further: jokes imply a return to childhood, to a time when playful jesting is not yet checked by inhibition. But jokes are also a vehicle for *discharging* psychical tension, hence the universal appeal these anecdotes have for Jews becomes revealing.

The Jewish marriage broker is a stock figure. There is the one who deceives subtly: "What!" exclaims the irate father. "You told me the girl's father was dead, and it turns out he's in prison." "You surely don't call that living," answers the matchmaker. Or the other *Schadchen* who brought along his assistant to echo the praises of the future bride: "She is straight as a pine tree," said the *Schadchen*. "As a pine tree," repeated the echo. "And she

has eyes that ought to be seen!" "What eyes she has!" confirmed the echo. "And she is better educated than anyone!" "What an education!" "It's true there's one thing," admitted the broker, "she has a small hump." "And *what* a hump!" the echo confirmed once more. Or the story of the bridegroom who, disagreeably surprised by his first glimpse of his betrothed, drew the broker aside and whispered: "Why have you brought me here? She's

ugly and old, she squints and has bad teeth and bleary eyes." "You needn't lower your voice," interrupted the broker, "she's deaf as well."

A master sophist tries to outwit a rabbi, but the rabbi is invested by his congregation with supernatural powers: praying among his disciples in Cracow, the rabbi suddenly utters a cry and announces the death of the rabbi at Lemberg. It is subsequently revealed that the latter is in

excellent health, but the disciples are not dissuaded by the detractors: "Whatever you may say, the *Kück* [look] from Cracow to Lemberg was a magnificent one." And the Establishment: imagine the idea of a Jew wanting to become a soldier. Nor is the business world overlooked: "But where's the Savior?" asks the art critic brought to admire two adjacent full-length portraits of a couple of unscrupulous businessmen.

The *Three Essays on the Theory of Sexuality* (1905) was a revolutionary publication and appeared at a time when most people believed in the sexual innocence of infants and children. But if there is such a thing as innocence among children it is to be found in their uncertain understanding of restrictive moral dictates, and nowhere else. In order to understand sexual perversions or fixations on infantile sexual activity, present to some degree among all adults, the path of sexual development has to be retraced back to its origins. Sexuality, to be sure, is not manifested fully developed at some point in growth, but is slowly prepared by the evolution of the *libido*, which is associated with all vital activities and frequently assumes an autoerotic character. The body is made up of many erotogenic zones, some more sensitive than others, and in particular those orifices concerned with nourishment and excretion. The search for knowledge itself is subject to the law of desire: children want to know where they come from, and their curiosity widens to include all natural phenomena. The discovery of their bodies and the world around them occurs simultaneously; ideally they transfer their interests to the external world, to outside objects, to other people, whose prototype in their eyes is obviously the parental couple. The "primal scene," whether witnessed or fantasied, offers the child distressing proof of the differences between the sexes. Children inevitably view coitus as a sadistic act, but sexual union also suggests the primary union, represented by the child's first dependence on its mother. And when a little girl repeats to her doll the same orders she has been given, she is at the same time both herself and her mother. Furthermore, the doll is usually marked with the stigma of excision, allaying the primary fear of punitive castration.

The theory of infantile sexuality was given clinical confirmation by the analysis of "little Hans," which Freud conducted by using the boy's father as intermediary. Some months after the birth of his little sister, the boy developed a phobia which prevented him from going outside for fear of being bitten by a horse. The "professor," as Freud was affectionately called by Hans, encouraged the father to explore openly the nature of his son's fundamentally Oedipal phantasm, and was able to discover a complex of impulses, including his masturbatory fascination with the male organ, concomitant scopophilia, and the infantile notion that all living beings possess a penis. At length, behind the fear of horses was revealed the boy's fear of his father. Struggling against the desire to bite/kill his father, Hans neurotically transformed his wish into the more passive and bearable phobia and at the same time displayed ample evidence of his fear of retaliation. The fact of having always "known" in his unconscious about the mystery of birth helped the child overcome his symptoms, and it was only necessary for him to understand the phenomenon in clear terms to be able to give up the idea of replacing his father. In the beginning, the transformation of Hans's libido into anxiety was projected onto the object of his phobia, the horse-father, on whose back he had played "giddyap." The pleasure of the sensation of movement, associated with desire for coitus with his mother, was inhibited by the neurosis; as a sort of secondary, if apparently contradictory, gain from his illness the shut-in child had the pleasure of remaining close to the object of his love. Even though he suffered no more than many other children, Hans had the opportunity of discovering his symptoms at the moment of crisis, thereby avoiding an adult neurosis resulting from years of repression.

The analysis of Hans was not the first of Freud's published case histories. Appearing in 1905, the "Fragment of an Analysis of a Case of Hysteria" dealt with the treatment in 1900 of a young middle-class girl named, for the occasion, Dora. The girl presented a number of somatic and mental symptoms, some of which, notably a persistent cough, seemed aimed at eliciting sympathy from those around her. The girl's father was in love with a woman who, according to Dora, was interested in him because he was "a man of fortune." Now, in German, "a man of *no* fortune" commonly means "an impotent man," and so by means of opposite representation, frequent among hysterics, Dora meant to convey that her father was sexually incapable. The contradiction of an impotent man having an affair was resolved with Dora's admission of her understanding of oral sex. A scandalous matter indeed, this disproportion between the professed virtues of the middle class and the confessions the physician brought forth in his discussion with the girl. Yet if the analysis was an admitted failure, it was not due to Freud's lack of interpretation, but rather to the *overdetermination* of the patient's symptoms, for it was revealed that Dora unconsciously and homosexually loved the same woman as her father, and in addition had been courted by the husband of her father's mistress, whose advances Dora rejected. Thus, it was as if the poor girl's libido had nowhere to turn. It was Dora's misfortune to feel that her father had traded her off in order to assure his own liaison: having already been treated by Freud for a nervous disorder, the father had brought him his daughter hoping thereby to ease his conscience. Since one of the characteristics of neurosis is the inability to reconcile the demands of reality with the fantasies of the unconscious, the case of Dora demonstrated how the wish for vengeance against the father can overshadow the desire to get well.

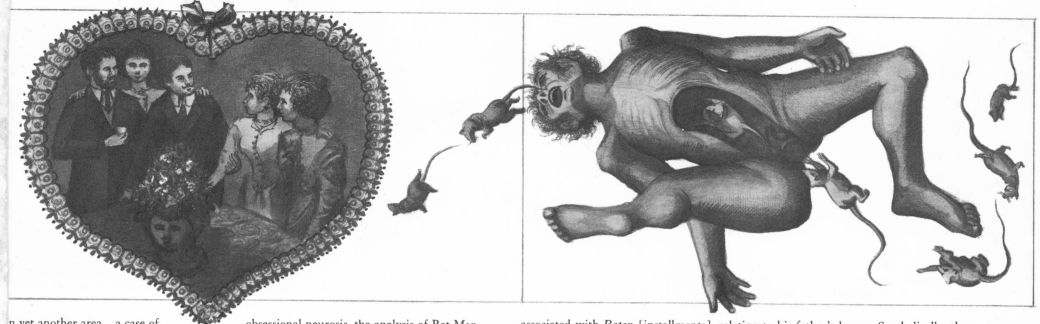

In yet another area, a case of obsessional neurosis, the analysis of Rat Man (1909) confirmed the 1905 theory of infantile sexuality and led Freud to modify his thesis to include the idea that "the unconscious *is* the infantile." The man in question, a reserve officer, suffered endless conflicts of feeling, represented by the diametrically opposed components of love and hate. The etiology of his agonizing delirium concerning rats could certainly be explained in part by early anal eroticism, aggravated by a case of childhood worms; but it was in the realm of language that the symptom was given its fullest dimension, for in his mind rats came to represent money: *Ratten* [rats] was

associated with *Raten* [installments], relating to his father's legacy. Symbolically, the rat represented the penis and venal love, as also it relates to children and money in the legend of the Pied Piper of Hamelin. Imprisoned in his own system of distortion by ellipsis, the patient in a real and painful manner made use of the same technique that gives many jokes their appeal. And through this juxtaposition of opposites, he revealed his hidden repression. Thus the Rat Man developed a syndrome of doubt and indecision to compensate for his death wish against his father. Although at the time Freud did not use the term, he was essentially describing the function of the *superego*.

Freud's commentary on the case of *Senatspräsident* Daniel Schreber, an appellate court judge, is not a genuine analysis, since it is based solely on the *Memoirs of a Neuropath*, published by Schreber in 1903, in which he recounts his paranoid delusions. Imagining himself the victim of homosexual assaults by his doctor, Schreber soon felt himself possessed by God, voluptuously, and believed he was destined to become a feminine savior of the world. Once again the father complex came into play, represented here as a struggle with God, "and his father's most dreaded threat, castration, actually provided the material for his wishful fantasy (at first resisted but later accepted) of being transformed into a woman."

In 1913 Freud ventured to correlate the three daughters in *King Lear*, the three caskets in *The Merchant of Venice* (interpreted as representing women), and the three choices confronting Paris in his celebrated judgment. What was the mythologic significance of choice based on this recurrent female triad? It was the juxtaposition of mother, wife, and Mother Earth: birth, love, and death. Thus among Lear's three daughters it is Cordelia who says the least; the lead casket that promises least; and Aphrodite who offers least. Consider also Cinderella and Psyche, who rank third after their older and more voluble sisters. Free choice, then, is nothing but illusion: ineluctable fate leads us all to our inevitable destiny.

The same curiosity concerning the hidden motives behind artistic creation led Freud in 1914 to write an article on Michelangelo's *Moses*. For years Freud had been obsessed by the figure of the historical Moses, and there is little doubt that the latter represented for him the image of the wrathful father. (Was not Freud himself one of Israel's disobedient sons?) Furthermore, the year 1914 marked Jung's defection; also, there was the association with Rome and Freud's friendship with Fliess. In his identification with Moses, Freud was seeking victory over his own passions concerning not only Jung's "heresy" but the rebellion of others who had already left him to worship the golden calf.

The case history of the Wolf Man (1914–1915) set forth the primacy of the libido over the influence of culture. When he was eighteen months old, the patient witnessed sexual intercourse between his parents, his father upright and his mother bent down like an animal. This was the source of his phobic obsession with wolves; it was as if his libido had been hopelessly splintered. Convinced *de visu* of the reality of castration, he developed an anxiety-neurosis which eventually made his relationship with his father difficult: he identified with his father concerning the supposed sadistic aspect of love, and in his masochism elected him as a sexual object. What remained in his conscious was fear not of the father but of the wolf.

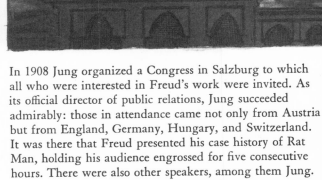

The polemical nature of the Wolf Man study signaled the final break between Freud and Jung in their theoretics. But it had taken years for this to happen. The two men first met in 1907, and the Swiss disciple, with boundless enthusiasm, considered his meeting with the master the most important event of his life. Freud went so far as to call the adherent from Zurich his "son and heir," and wrote him that he was the Joshua destined to explore the promised land of psychoanalysis while he, Freud, like Moses, would only view it from afar. It is possible that at fifty-one, Freud felt the need to appoint a successor capable of bringing the new-found theories to fruition, and so he chose this man of "original mind" in whom he saw all the qualities of a leader: vitality, decisiveness, unrestrained imagination, and above all outstanding qualifications as a psychiatrist.

In 1908 Jung organized a Congress in Salzburg to which all who were interested in Freud's work were invited. As its official director of public relations, Jung succeeded admirably: those in attendance came not only from Austria but from England, Germany, Hungary, and Switzerland. It was there that Freud presented his case history of Rat Man, holding his audience engrossed for five consecutive hours. There were also other speakers, among them Jung.

I still think there's more to it than sexuality.

The Jew from Vienna was overjoyed to have rallied to his cause the *goyim* from Zurich who were the most widely respected practitioners of mental hygiene. At the end of the meeting, through the efforts of Eugen Bleuler, plans were made to issue the first periodical devoted to psychoanalysis. Jung, Freud's junior by twenty-five years, was chosen as its editor.

The devoted Karl Abraham, who had at one time worked with Jung in Switzerland, complained of the latter's fondness for astrology and mysticism, which criticism Freud rejected as unfounded. Yet with time Freud would change his mind. Meanwhile, although convinced that Jung was still the "man of the future," he did voice his displeasure concerning the young man's devotion to research in mythology, and bade him "to return to the neuroses, the motherland of psychoanalysis, regardless of the interest of her colonies."

But the distance between them began to increase. Jung routinely rejected the idea of discussing with patients unsavory details of their intimate life. His discretion was deemed a weakness masquerading as virtue, a good example of the physician's resistance to his own impulses. Soon Jung was publicly affirming his doubts about sexual etiology. But Freud remained deaf to the rumors regarding his chosen heir.

He was more interested in having psychoanalysis serve as a common meeting ground for scientists and practitioners than as a melting pot for the reshaping of theories. He dreamed of ecumenical harmony, and for a time Jung nourished his utopian hopes. In 1908 Freud was invited to America to give a series of lectures at Clark University, all expenses paid. He was elated by the prospect of the trip: he was looking forward to seeing the magnificent collection of Cyprian antiquities in New York; Sandor Ferenczi would accompany him, and Jung himself had been invited. The three men would make the trip together. They met in Bremen, had an excellent crossing, and amused themselves during the trip by analyzing each other's dreams. Following the obligatory visits to museums and his initial contact with American gigantism, Freud began preparing his *Five Lectures on Psycho-Analysis*. The lectures were adapted for an audience of nonprofessionals and were given without notes. Freud himself thought they were "old hat"; but when the series ended he expressed joy at seeing his efforts finally recognized. His impressions of America were not favorable, however: American pragmatism was assuredly ill suited to the doctrine of psychoanalysis.

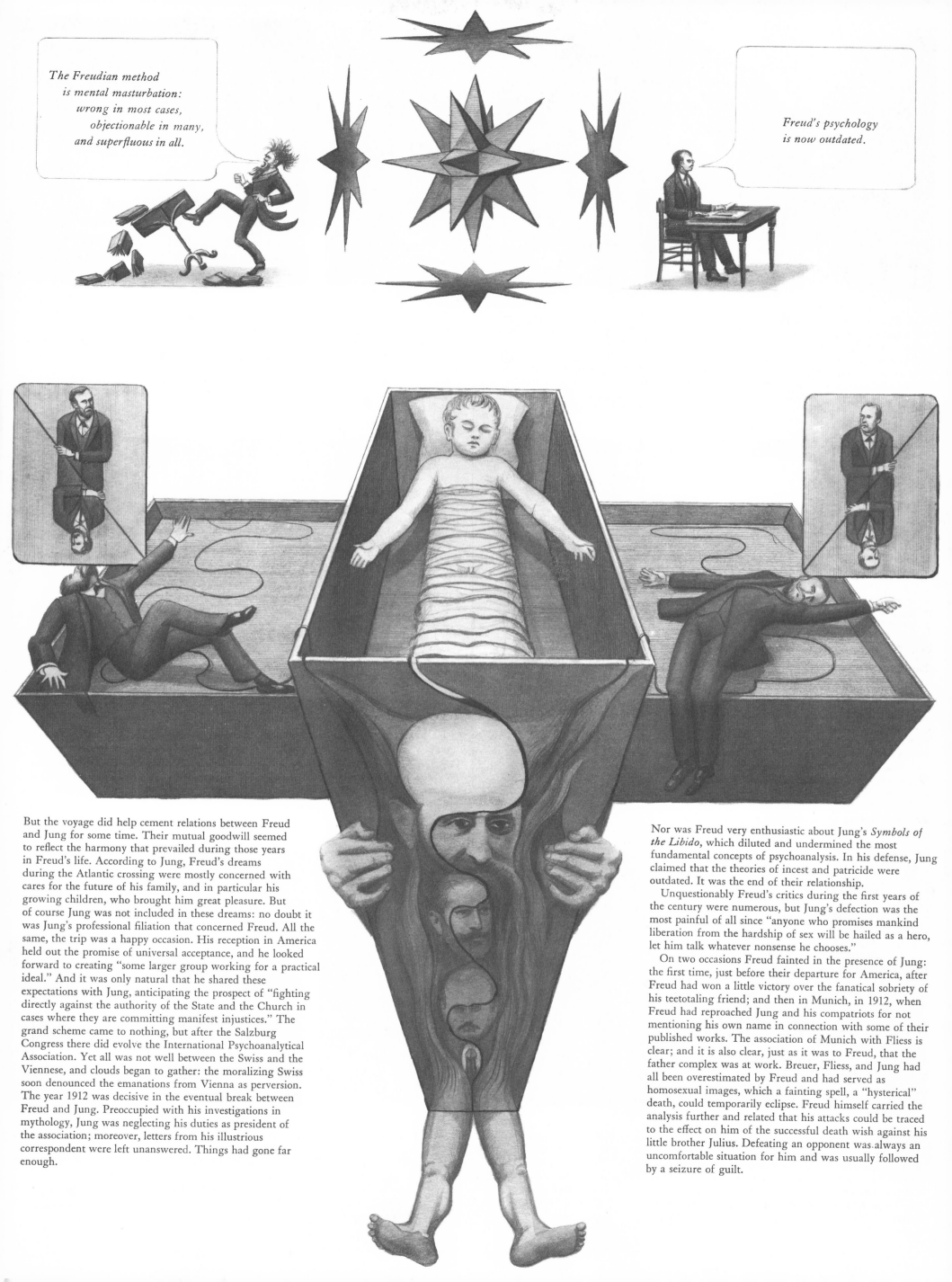

But the voyage did help cement relations between Freud and Jung for some time. Their mutual goodwill seemed to reflect the harmony that prevailed during those years in Freud's life. According to Jung, Freud's dreams during the Atlantic crossing were mostly concerned with cares for the future of his family, and in particular his growing children, who brought him great pleasure. But of course Jung was not included in these dreams: no doubt it was Jung's professional filiation that concerned Freud. All the same, the trip was a happy occasion. His reception in America held out the promise of universal acceptance, and he looked forward to creating "some larger group working for a practical ideal." And it was only natural that he shared these expectations with Jung, anticipating the prospect of "fighting directly against the authority of the State and the Church in cases where they are committing manifest injustices." The grand scheme came to nothing, but after the Salzburg Congress there did evolve the International Psychoanalytical Association. Yet all was not well between the Swiss and the Viennese, and clouds began to gather: the moralizing Swiss soon denounced the emanations from Vienna as perversion. The year 1912 was decisive in the eventual break between Freud and Jung. Preoccupied with his investigations in mythology, Jung was neglecting his duties as president of the association; moreover, letters from his illustrious correspondent were left unanswered. Things had gone far enough.

Nor was Freud very enthusiastic about Jung's *Symbols of the Libido*, which diluted and undermined the most fundamental concepts of psychoanalysis. In his defense, Jung claimed that the theories of incest and patricide were outdated. It was the end of their relationship.

Unquestionably Freud's critics during the first years of the century were numerous, but Jung's defection was the most painful of all since "anyone who promises mankind liberation from the hardship of sex will be hailed as a hero, let him talk whatever nonsense he chooses."

On two occasions Freud fainted in the presence of Jung: the first time, just before their departure for America, after Freud had won a little victory over the fanatical sobriety of his teetotaling friend; and then in Munich, in 1912, when Freud had reproached Jung and his compatriots for not mentioning his own name in connection with some of their published works. The association of Munich with Fliess is clear; and it is also clear, just as it was to Freud, that the father complex was at work. Breuer, Fliess, and Jung had all been overestimated by Freud and had served as homosexual images, which a fainting spell, a "hysterical" death, could temporarily eclipse. Freud himself carried the analysis further and related that his attacks could be traced to the effect on him of the successful death wish against his little brother Julius. Defeating an opponent was always an uncomfortable situation for him and was usually followed by a seizure of guilt.

During the first year of their friendship, Jung had called Freud's attention to *Gradiva*, a short novel by the contemporary Danish writer Wilhelm Jensen. As he had already done with Shakespeare, Freud applied his analytic method to this fictional narrative, concerned more with finding confirmation of his theories than in gaining insights into the unconscious. Of particular interest to Freud was the story's oneiric theme, which seemed justifiably to assign the artist's work of fantasy to the jurisdiction of psychoanalysis. Freud's detailed and subtle analysis of the tale might well have elicited the same wonderment he felt at his discoveries in the human psychism: "I can hardly bring myself to believe it yet. It is as if Schliemann had dug up another Troy which had hitherto been believed to be mythical."

The young hero of *Gradiva*, himself an archeologist, becomes enamored of a bas-relief of a Grecian girl, represented by her creator with a particularly graceful gait. The young man is convinced beyond doubt that the girl had lived in Pompeii and was buried during the famous eruption that engulfed the city. In defiance of reality he is driven by his delusion to that spot where she must still be. But before leaving his hometown, and without his being aware of it, in the street he passes his childhood playmate,

the woman he really loves and who in turn loves him. By one of those convenient coincidences permitted in fiction, he meets this same woman in Pompeii. While the young lady attempts to bring him to his senses, the hero persists in his delusion that he has found his phantom love. Thus the "fetishistic" displacement of his affective attachment to the bas-relief was merely an attempt to conceal his repressed love for his childhood playmate turned therapist, and in whom the reader recognizes the mysterious

incarnation. The hero's erotic impulse underwent the same "archeologic" fate as his beloved sculpture: suppression under the ashes of traumatism rather than actual destruction.

Freud admired Jensen's penetrating insights and wrote him for confirmation of his views; the author at first merely replied politely and noncommittally. In Jung's opinion, Jensen's work pointed to an early incestuous love

between brother and sister. Freud went further and postulated that the foot fetishism—*Gradiva* means "the walker"—was simply the fictional transposition of a real infirmity in some girl Jensen had loved. As a young boy he must have grieved over the sickness or perhaps death of his sister, or some other girl, and the circumstance was obliterated through his creative imagination. Subsequently, Jensen partly confirmed this view, telling Freud that his

first love had been a little girl with whom he had grown up and who died of tuberculosis when she was eighteen; and that he later fell in love with another girl who resembled the first and who died suddenly in the bloom of youth. Although Freud's hypothesis was not wrong, it neglected the important factor of *displacement* in artistic creativity, also common to dreams, wherein one element suggests another in the same register as the first.

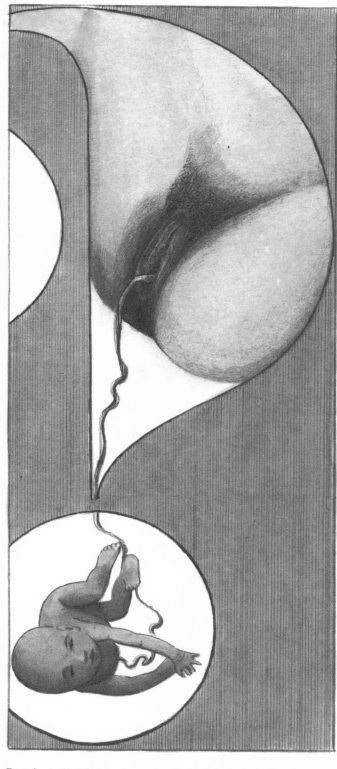

Jung's influence is again apparent in Freud's *Leonardo da Vinci and a Memory of his Childhood*, published in 1910. Here the master is clearly interested in exploring the manifestation of human impulses within the context of civilization, as opposed to the more restricted study offered by clinical case histories. The analytic biography of the great painter is based on his single recorded childhood memory, in which he recounts that when he was in his cradle a mysterious bird, a kite or vulture, came down to him and opened his mouth with its tail. Again, it was not the creative process that concerned Freud, rather the forces of environment wherein he could exercise his analytical idiom and reconstruct da Vinci's destiny from the starting point of an illusion.

For in fact Freud set aside the question of inspiration and chose to interpret Leonardo's cradle memory as a symbolic fantasy arising from the unconscious. The suggestion of a father complex is revealed in da Vinci's repeated insistence that he was the *father* of his own works. As for the fantasy, it was an ambiguous representation of both the penis and the breast. The artist's attitude toward his paintings, frequently left unfinished, reflects his father's

treatment of him. Even his inhibitory inability to create was associated with his father, for he did not dare surpass his procreator. His need for partners of the same sex was a result of his mother's excessive devotion, which made him, the male, the model love-object. And by dedicating his works to his mother, he compensated her for having been abandoned by his father.

Paradoxically, despite his exceptional life, da Vinci's career, like that of any lesser mortal, was marked by a certain determinism. A child is always curious about the mysteries of sexuality, and this insatiable need to understand can develop in three ways: it can be quickly arrested, thereby inhibiting the activity of intelligence; it can be linked with the search for knowledge in general,

the *libidinization* of thinking itself, with the accompanying pleasure and anxiety related to the sexual process; or this epistemophilic curiosity can, through *sublimation,* dissociate itself from sexuality and become pure intellectual drive. It was the subtle blending of these last two effects that produced the complex and prodigious creator of *La Gioconda*. According to Freud "only a man who had had

Leonardo's childhood experience could have painted the Mona Lisa and the St. Anne, have secured so melancholy a fate for his works and have embarked on such an astonishing career as a natural scientist, as if the key to all his achievements and misfortunes lay hidden in the childhood fantasy of the vulture." Such unsanctification of creative genius seemed almost sacrilegious.

This somewhat naïve interpretation was in fact carried further by his Swiss colleagues, who, eager to point out Freud's limitations, discovered the outline of a vulture in the painting of St. Anne, claiming thereby to put the fantasy into the realm of reality. It was undoubtedly this sort of willful and at times tragic misunderstanding that led the Nazis years later to burn Freud's books, calling them a kind of "lucubration of the Jewish spirit."

Freud's research into anthropologic data derived from the dynamics of the unconscious, and gave evidence of the unity of his diversity. *Totem and Taboo*, published in 1913, lies along the path that was first taken in 1899 with *The Interpretation of Dreams* and ended in 1938 with *Moses and Monotheism*. In the earliest work Freud describes the wish to kill one's father; in the other two the wish becomes deed. And the moral consequence of the original murder, repeated and absolved through sacrificial ceremony, became the establishment of a social order made possible by the law against incest.

Order in the totemic system was based on the dual prohibition against killing and eating the totem, and against sexual relations between members of the same totem. This clear-cut law of ancient times became more or less corrupted by civilization, but it still persists deep inside us all. Freud postulated that the original chieftain of humanity was a jealous male who in his desire to keep all females for himself prevented any younger men from approaching them sexually.

The influence of Darwin is of course evident. Yet primitive men must have recognized in the totem the symbol of the murdered ancestral father. And here the experience of psychoanalysis suggested the hypothesis that the totemic sacrifice compensated for what was forbidden to each by permitting it to all. The animal was killed by all, mourned by all, and thus the responsibility for the murder was no one's; it was then eaten, and the festival that followed celebrated the triumph over hostile forces. "The importance which is everywhere, without exception, ascribed to sacrifice lies in the fact that it offers satisfaction to the father for the outrage inflicted on him in the same act in which that deed is commemorated."

It was thus that the sons obtained the coveted totem, but to avoid any recurrence of the crime a pact was quickly made which prohibited access to the women, reminders of the all-powerful father.

One taboo in particular interested Freud and confirmed the idea of emotional ambivalence. Among certain tribes, slain enemy warriors were treated with great consideration; the severed heads were given dainty morsels of food and forgiveness was implored. Thus the whole seems to be represented by one of its parts, and the slaying becomes associated with castration. Also, Freud the clinician remembered that children (the example of "little Hans") frequently choose as their phobic object an animal symbolic of the father, who is both hated and loved. Therefore it is not unreasonable to assume that the choice of an animal victim as the best means of appeasing the father was the unconscious representation of the paternal penis; and so also the offering of one's own children, who symbolize the fruits of virility, as in the sacrifice of Isaac by Abraham and Iphigenia by Agamemnon. Finally, what is sacrificed is the power of procreation. Is not the original meaning of the word *sacrifice* both "sanctify" and "anathematize"?

The question of the religious beliefs of the "Godless Jew," as Freud was pleased to call himself, was in part settled with the appearance of his cherished *Totem and Taboo*. Yet the book must also be seen as a personal reaction to Jung's *Symbols of the Libido*, with which Freud disagreed. "Jung is crazy," he wrote to Ferenczi, "but I don't really want a split; I should prefer him to leave on his own accord. Perhaps my *Totem* work will hasten the break against my will."

It was in part his disagreement with Jung and Adler that led Freud to modify his metapsychology to include a new concept of the ego. The new component, essential in all affective activity, was self-love, or *narcissism*, which may be traced to the origin of the organism, when it is totally invested in itself. This primitive state is manifested in severe cases of pathology, such as sexual perversion or psychosis, where the ego precludes any exterior investment of the libido. Even in the ordinary matter of selecting a partner, narcissism is at work, advising us to choose a love-object that corresponds with the picture we have of ourselves, or of what we used to be or would like to be.

The formation of self-love is necessarily shaped by ego-investment, which is indispensable in enabling the subject to differentiate itself from a succession of mirror-images wherein the final limitation is revealed: the impossibility of one of its token parts, the phallus, representing the whole.

On Narcissism: An Introduction (1914) initiated a series of works of prime importance concerning theory. Fetishism, for example, according to Freud, is a way of responding to the fear of castration. Repudiating the evidence of reality, the fetishist refuses to recognize the absence of a penis in women. He thus chooses some object that will serve as an acceptable substitute for the maternal penis, devoting himself to it religiously. Denying the difference between the sexes is the surest protection against the loss of one's own penis and the attendant threat to narcissism.

The terror that comes over the little boy at the sight of the frightening hirsute maternal fissure has its counterpart in mythology in the snaky-haired Medusa, who "petrified" all those who viewed her. The advantage gained by the fetishist is real: he bypasses homosexuality, because in his eyes women are endowed with the necessary attributes to make them suitable sexual objects. For this reason pieces of underclothing are often chosen as a fetish, since they "crystallize the moment of undressing, the last moment in which the woman [can] still be regarded as phallic." Freud maintained that the fetishist's belief is simultaneously disavowed and affirmed: "Although it is true that women have no penis, they still must really have one." And this obvious illogicality constitutes a genuine *splitting of the ego.*

It was in 1923, in what might be called his "new topography," that Freud proposed the division of mental personality into three entities whose functions, although differentiated, are all rooted in the unconscious. The new schema did not nullify the former distinction among the concepts of the conscious, the preconscious, and the unconscious, but did however refine the distinction in light of his clinical discoveries. The new system included the notion of a great reservoir of psychical energy associated with the libido and with Freud's newly formulated *death instinct*, a hypothesis that was to reappear with increasing frequency. This completely instinctual primordial reservoir of energy was called the id. The ego, in part unconscious, acts as a buffer between reality and the id: "it yields only too readily to the temptation of becoming a base flatterer. . . . In the process of identification and sublimation, it lends support to the death instinct, siding with the id in opposition to the libido, but in so doing runs the risk of itself becoming the object of the death instinct. In order to be effective the ego must be invested by the libido so as to work in the service of Eros, thus desiring to live and to be loved." Separate from the ego, and also unconscious in part, is the superego, the critical agency established by the internalization of prohibitions, which exercises harsh moral control.

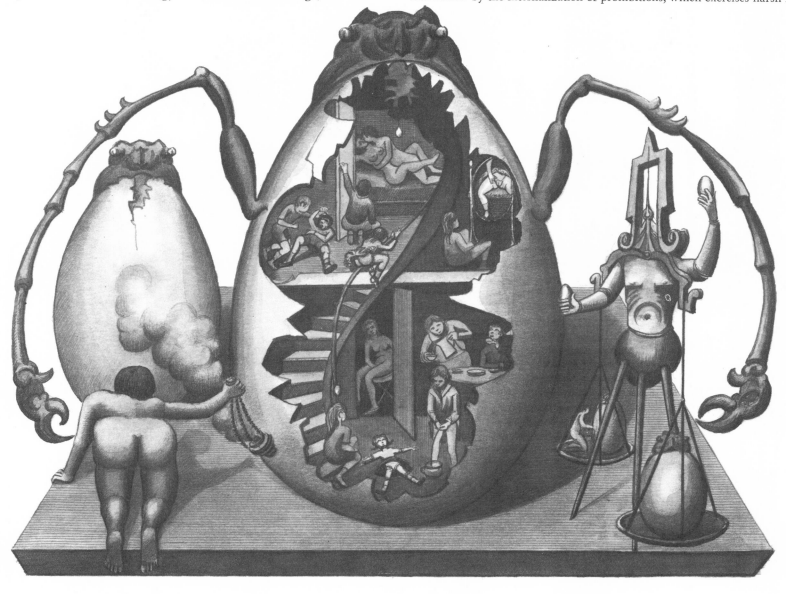

While observing one of his grandsons at play, Freud became aware that the "o" sound the child made each time he threw a wooden spool from his crib represented the German word *fort* ("gone"), and that his joyful *da* ("there"), when he was once again in possession of the spool, signaled its return. The game was repeatedly acted out and its interpretation was clear: the disappearance and reappearance of the spool represented his mother's departure and her return. It was also clear that a painful event, normally accompanied by screams and tears, was by its very repetition transformed into one of pleasure, and indirectly marked a feeling of triumph over absence and want. What Freud would henceforth call the *repetition-compulsion* allowed him to incorporate into his theory the possibility of the symbolic transformation of raw impressions, obliquely through language, from the "primary process" to the "secondary" or ideational process.

Nietzsche's doctrine of the "eternal recurrence of the same" was familiar to Freud, and beginning in 1920, with the introduction of his famous death instinct theory based on the repetition-compulsion, he suggested the importance of a *primary masochism*: the direct action on the self of the death instinct, before it has been turned outward in the form of aggression. The universal tendency toward mutilation, directed by the destructive force of guilt, led to the question of explaining how pain can be transformed into pleasure. Its symbolic representation was demonstrated by the child's game with the spool; however, the impulse of the death instinct precedes such activity and puts the ego in the position of being the object of narcissistic investment, which counterbalances the drive toward self-destruction.

Using the well-known myth that Plato has Aristophanes recount in the *Symposium*, Freud gave some idea of the opposition between the destructive tendency in the death instinct and the libidinal energy that strives for union and harmony. The androgynous ball was our original form and it was owing to a prank of the irreverent Zeus that we became separated into men and women (does not the word *sex* itself derive from *secare*, "to divide"?). Since then we have not ceased in our search for that lost unity. And the rational basis of our nostalgia for union can perhaps even be traced to the trauma of birth, a separation mandated by life, but opposed by the desire to return to the place of our origin.

Love-Strife

It was again in Greek thought, but pre-Socratic this time, that Freud found an illustration of this dialectic: φιλία and νεῖχος ("love" and "strife") embody in the form of another allegory the universal division into the two opposing principles that rule the world. It is not surprising that the speculations of metapsychology borrowed from the precepts of philosophy; but it is worth noting, however,

that in Freud's encounter with metaphysics he relegates himself to the fringes of occidental thinking, as if he were unable to remain within the confines of the accepted academic *logos*. And so he indulges in the ramblings of the half-drunk Aristophanes, the poetry of Empedocles, and the fulminations of that other certified adversary of Socrates, the more modern but equally Dionysian

Nietzsche. Here is what the latter wrote in his *Genealogy of Morals* concerning the origins of "bad conscience": "The whole inner world burst apart when man's external outlets became *obstructed*. These terrible bulwarks, with which the social organization protected itself against the old instincts of freedom—punishments belong preeminently to these bulwarks—brought it about that all

those instincts of wild, free, prowling man became turned backwards, *against man himself*. Enmity, cruelty, the delight in persecution, in surprises, change, destruction—the turning of all these instincts against their own possessors: this was the origin of the 'bad conscience.' It was man who, lacking external enemies and obstacles, and imprisoned as he was in the oppressive narrowness and monotony of custom, in his own impatience lacerated,

persecuted, gnawed, frightened, and ill-treated himself; it was this animal in the hands of the tamer which beat itself against the bars of its cage; it was this being who, pining and yearning for that desert home of which it had been deprived, was compelled to create out of its own self an adventure, a torture chamber, a hazardous and perilous desert; it was this fool, this homesick and desperate prisoner, who invented the 'bad conscience.'"

Whether on the subject of religion (*The Future of an Illusion*, 1927) or in the field of sociology (*Civilization and Its Discontents*, 1930), Freud is careful to draw our attention to the evolving myths that provide the mortar of any society and in which its ideals are firmly fixed. Along with the materialist philosopher Ludwig Feuerbach, Freud might have said: "Religion is the dream of waking consciousness; dreaming is the key to the mysteries of religion."

For the average man religion is nothing but "a system of doctrines and promises which on the one hand explains to him the riddles of the world with enviable completeness, and, on the other, assures him that a careful Providence will watch over his life and will compensate him in a future existence for any frustrations he suffers here. The common man cannot imagine this Providence otherwise than in the figure of an enormously exalted father. Only

such a being can understand the needs of the children of men and be softened by their prayers and placated by the signs of their remorse."

Likewise, in *Civilization and Its Discontents*, Freud sees the fundamental social conflict as the result of "a primary mutual hostility which turns men one against the other, so that civilization has to use its utmost efforts in order to set limits to man's aggressive instincts." In both areas, religion

and social ethics, the role played by the superego is evident: whether in the psychology of the group or of the individual neurotic, a sense of guilt is the organism's specific response to repressed aggression. And the undisguised objective of religion is to regulate those human relations which the moral dictates of civilization alone cannot guarantee.

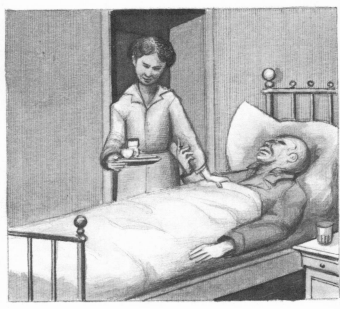

The years during which Freud elaborated his concept of the death instinct coincided with a major turning point in his life. The year 1923 marked not only a new departure for Freud with the publication of *The Ego and the Id*, but the onset of the fatal cancer that would require thirty-three operations during the remaining sixteen years of his life. In addition to his deteriorating physical state during those years, Freud was plagued by the loss of loved ones within

his own family and the loss of collaborators within the family of psychoanalysis, either by death or defection. The jealous father did not always view with favor the efforts of younger men to slay him, even if only in theory. The details of the internal dynamics of the group are too many to recount: some turned away because of mental illness, others turned to heresy, easily explained by the frequently defined principle of transference. Those who remained

with him were all the more cherished. First among these was his daughter Anna, born in 1896, who became her father's indispensable nurse. Following an attack of angina pectoris in the street, the inveterate smoker could no longer ignore the deleterious effects of tobacco. His disciple Ferenczi offered to analyze him in an effort to help him cure the habit, but, alluding to his own advanced years, Freud declined.

And so our little town, henceforth renowned throughout Moravia, has the distinct honor of . . .

Despite the discretion, or at times lack of courage, on the part of his doctors, Freud soon realized that his malignancy was incurable. He calmly accepted his impending death—although it was still years away—and took comfort in the fact that in his last hours he would be surrounded by friends. His fame was now secure, but recognition had an ambivalent effect on the ill and aging man. He could not help feeling flattered by the universal

dissemination of psychoanalysis, but at the same time resented the attention given his person, as though he surmised therein a resistance to the theories of psychoanalysis. The founder of the doctrine, the man, was honored and praised; but what about the doctrine itself? The homage paid him as a Jew or a Viennese, for example, however exalted the motive, left him indifferent when the approbation was not directed to the

psychoanalytical movement. Thus he began to dread notoriety. He was discussed in newspapers (an American paper even reported that he was slowly dying); a sculptor made a full-length statue of him; in Freiberg a bronze plaque was placed on the house in which he was born; and his birthdays were marked by eulogies and an endless flow of telegrams from all over the world. In 1927 Einstein paid him a visit.

The idea is madness. I want no honors bestowed on me.

Many well-intentioned people made efforts to win for him the Nobel Prize. Shortly before his eightieth birthday he wrote indignantly to Marie Bonaparte: "The rumors that reach me about preparations for my birthday annoy me as much as the newspaper gossip about a Nobel Prize. I am not easily deceived, and I know that the attitude of the world toward me and my work is really no friendlier than twenty years ago." But his correspondent was not dissuaded; and she remained

one of his favorites among those who brought him cheer during the last years of his life. This chaste man who remained faithful to Martha, his only love, had made several lasting friendships among women in whom he recognized a sublimated loving affection. His own relationship with Marie Bonaparte, the somewhat masculine Greek princess who was studying analysis, was assuredly intellectual. Yet she was only one of a

series of female companions which included Minna Bernays, his sister-in-law; Joan Riviere, a disciple from England; and above all Lou Andreas-Salomé, who enlisted in the ranks beginning with the Congress of 1911. She had a flair for great men: Nietzsche, Rilke, Rodin, and Strindberg were among her friends. She had also known both Turgenev and Tolstoy. Her death in 1937 was a considerable loss to Freud.

Death was all around him. Foreshadowing his own departure, his mother died in 1930, at the age of ninety-five, after suffering complications that required the constant use of morphine. But wisdom had worked its way on the septuagenarian and he was able to analyze the event with some detachment: "Assuredly, there is no saying, what effects such an experience may produce in deeper layers, but on the surface I can detect only two things: an increase in personal freedom, since it was always a terrifying thought that she might come to hear of my death; and secondly, the satisfaction that at last she has achieved the deliverance for which she had earned a right after such a long life."

Shortly before his mother's death, Freud learned that he had been awarded the Goethe prize. The honor gave him great pleasure because of his admiration for the man. The ceremony—which his illness prevented him from attending—took place in Frankfurt with Anna reading his prepared speech, whose theme was the justification of applying the techniques of psychoanalysis to the study of great men, and in particular a man like Goethe who had such keen insight into the depths of the human mind.

Our brave government is defending us, but quien sabe? *I can only say, along with Meister Anton in Hebbel's drama: "I no longer understand this world."*

During the last years in Vienna, in the close circle of his family, the patriarch resigned himself to his physical suffering, devoting his time to the synthesis of his ideas, with occasional visits to the countryside. Thus he found not only diversion from his illness but a convenient retreat from an increasingly disquieting political situation. Growing old and in semiretirement, Freud gave some indication of his uncertainty in a letter of 1937 addressed to Marie Bonaparte, who had just sent him the manuscript of a book she had written on dogs, animals for which they both had much affection: "Your manuscript just arrived. I love it. . . . It is, of course, not an analytic work, but the analyst's search for truth and knowledge can be perceived behind this creation. It really gives the real reasons for the remarkable fact that one can love an animal . . . so deeply: affection without any ambivalence, the simplicity of life free from the conflicts of civilization that are so hard to endure, the beauty of an existence complete in itself. . . . When you at a youthful fifty-four cannot avoid thinking of death, you cannot be astonished that at the age of eighty and a half I fret whether I shall reach the age of my father and brother or further still into my mother's age, tormented . . . [as I am] by the conflict between the wish for rest and the dread of fresh suffering. . . ."

How did Jews come to be what they are?

The conflicts of civilization! As early as 1933, beginning with the Reichstag fire, friends urged Freud to leave Vienna to escape the Nazi menace. But his reasons for staying were numerous and would only grow stronger with time: "It is not certain," he wrote to Ferenczi, "that the Hitler regime will master Austria too. That is possible, it is true, but everybody believes it will not attain the crudeness of brutality here that it has in Germany. There is no personal danger for me, and when you picture life with the suppression of us Jews as extremely unpleasant do not forget what an uncomfortable life settling abroad, whether in Switzerland or England, promises for refugees. . . . besides, if they were to slay one it is simply one kind of death like another."

How much had changed since the first International Congress in 1909! By the mid-1930s Abraham and Ferenczi were dead, and many of his associates had emigrated to America. Of the original Committee, Ernest Jones was the only member remaining in Europe. It was his intervention that proved decisive, in both Vienna and London, when Freud finally consented to leave. Meanwhile, Freud lived with his false hopes; yet despite the events of history he was able to start work on the book that was to occupy him to the end: *Moses and Monotheism.*

In Freud's last creative effort, published in 1939, he returned to the subject of the relationship between religious ideology and repression. Although the work was prompted by the passing circumstance of history, it became his final statement before entering history himself.

An Egyptian named Moses, who had adopted the monotheistic doctrine of a sun-worshipping pharaoh, left his country in exile taking with him a tribe of immigrant slaves, "chosen" by himself, to whom he taught the rite of circumcision and the cult of a single divine being. He was later put to death when his people rebelled against him. The subsequent sense of guilt experienced by these Jews for having killed the "primal father" resulted in their tracing their monotheism back to Abraham, and in replacing the slain leader by another Moses, this one a mild and patient man and a disciple of Yahweh, a local volcano god. Another consequence of the rejection of the Egyptian Moses was the recurring wish for a new Messiah, through whom the original crime might be expiated; and it was thus that Christianity was born. The persistent hostility of the Jewish prophets to idolatry was a result of the conflict between the unadulterated monotheism that came out of Egypt and the degenerate paganism represented by the other Moses who had joined forces with the Jews at the time of the exodus. The experience of trauma, however, was felt only by those Jews who followed the first Moses. Gradually the concept of a single divinity

triumphed over the worship of spurious gods, prompted by the wish that the murdered Moses would return. This yearning found its most poignant expression in Saint Paul, who promulgated the idea of original sin (the murder) and the redemption of the crime against the Father through the death of the Son.

In this last work, Freud provided a key to the virulent anti-Semitism among Christians, present in every period of history and especially in his own. At the outset Christianity was a religion of love, but over the years it retrogressed, as if the disciples of polytheism had won a cyclic victory over the spiritual virtue of the Egyptian pharaoh Akhnaton. The fundamental reproach made by Christians against Jews stems from one basic difference: "You won't *admit* that you murdered God. It is true, we did the same thing, but we *admitted* it, and since then we have been purified." Freud's abiding interest in the figure of Moses was urgently renewed by the Nazi persecutions, causing him to wonder what constitutes the basis of hate that produced such violent reactions against a people who for reasons real or imagined were universally set apart. Life in Vienna had become intolerable. With the recollection of the burning of his books in Berlin some years earlier, Freud witnessed the German invasion of Austria on March 12, 1938. His work on Moses would draw opposition from all sides: from scholars, from Catholics, and in particular from Jews, who labeled him a renegade.

Meanwhile, his "dear old cancer," using the condemned man's own term, got progressively worse. Max Schur, Freud's doctor since 1928, described in a series of notes the long ordeal involving operations, prostheses, and radium treatment that went on unceasingly, in Vienna as

well as abroad. Although tormented by pain, Freud was always patient and refused any drug except for an occasional aspirin. His interest in the outside world never diminished; he was concerned for the health of his family and friends and went on analyzing patients to the very

end. Also, his lifelong habit of letter writing continued unabated. The last book he was able to read was, symptomatically, Balzac's *La Peau de chagrin*. Never a humorless man, he gave evidence of his wit up to the last: "Like a hungry dog I'm waiting for a promised

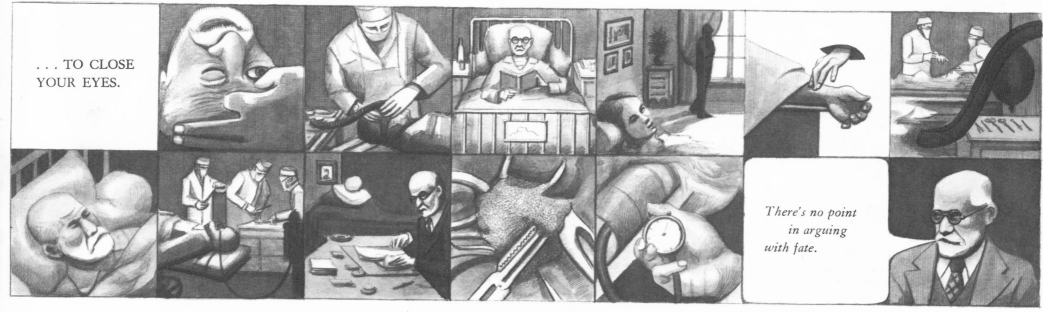

. . . TO CLOSE YOUR EYES.

There's no point in arguing with fate.

bone; but the bone, it seems, is really my own." "Do you think this will be the last war?" Schur asked him. "Anyhow, *my* last war," he replied. And again to Schur, whose wife's pregnancy had gone several days beyond term: "You are going from a man who doesn't want to leave the world to a child who doesn't want to come into it."

Arrangements for Freud's self-imposed exile involved the efforts of many. Help came, however, from two unexpected quarters: from Mussolini, who requested that the exit visa be granted; and from Dr. Sauerwald, a fervent anti-Semitic Nazi commissar, who, in remembrance of his admiration for one of Freud's Jewish colleagues, eased some of the

administrative difficulties with the Nazi regime. Less surprising was the intervention of Ambassador Bullitt, who prevailed upon his personal friend President Roosevelt to contact the German ambassador in Washington and insist on the importance of treating Freud well.

The mediations, some official, others officious, required zeal. Efforts were coordinated by Ernest Jones, who had already expertly facilitated the emigration of other Viennese psychiatrists. After the *Anschluss,* negotiations became more difficult, but in the end Jones prevailed. The venerable man was received triumphantly by the British, who deemed it an honor to harbor one of the great

thinkers of the century. Their expression of genuine consideration and respect helped alleviate the inevitable pain of exile and the physical suffering caused by his increasingly weakened state. Freud had lived in the same city for seventy-nine years. He had celebrated his golden wedding anniversary in the same house where shortly after his marriage he had brought his young bride.

His ashes repose in a Grecian urn in a country not his own, but which felt privileged to offer him asylum. Legend tells the story of yet another man, who, attended by his faithful daughter, was driven away to die. He abandoned Thebes and wandered to Colonus, where, it was decreed, the possession of his body would bring the city joy:

his name was Oedipus.

Michel Siméon was born in 1920 and studied engraving with Albert Flocon and Freiandler. He was associated with André Breton and the Surrealists as well as with Jacques Prévert and his group. His illustrations have appeared in many books and magazines published in France and his work is in the collection of the Museum of Modern Art in Paris. The drawings for this book were executed in graphite and wash.

Robert Ariel was born in 1939. He has taught linguistics at the University of Paris (Nanterre) and at the University of Abidjan (Ivory Coast). He has translated books on linguistics and logic from English into French and is the author of several scholarly works linking linguistics and psychoanalysis.

FREUD

The Psychoanalytic Adventure